"Hope Fully is for anyone who has ever wrestled with disappointment, pain, and unfulfilled desires and wondered how to trust God in the midst of it. It is also —one might argue even more so—for anyone who is still in it: in the mess, in the grief, in the in-between. If this is you, get ready for your heart to collide with a whole lot of truth and a whole lot more gentleness and grace. Amie shares her story with the tone of a close friend catching up with you over a cup of coffee and asking you, "But how are you really doing?" because she is the real deal. Her unapologetic honesty as well as compassion, kindness, boldness, wisdom, and warmth is exactly what you will experience if you spend time with her in real life (and she'd love nothing more than to do just that with you!). I highly recommend this book.

— TAIKO BENNETT, AUTHOR

HOPE FULLY

AMIE BETH

Published by Amie Beth

www.amiebeth.com

Library of Congress Control Number: 2020915749

Paperback ISBN: 978-1-7355813-0-9

Ebook ISBN: 978-1-7355813-1-6

Cover Design by Amie Beth

CONTENTS

FOREWORD

"I think I see the Matterhorn."

We were a mere five miles into a two hundred and fifteen mile trip, but hope was springing up from the little girl with pig tails in the back seat. Hope that caused her heart to see what was promised long before her physical eyes beheld that mountain standing tall amidst the magic kingdom.

This is but one moment her mother and I deeply treasure. We have watched Amie develop from birth into a remarkable daughter, woman, mother, friend, neighbor, businesswoman, author, and who knows what else to come. The woman does not stop. She's full of faith, love, and hope. All of it keeps her moving toward what others have not seen—*yet*.

Amie comes from a long line of those who have encountered the most difficult of times, events, and people. In 1894, her then fourteen-year-old great grandfather left a difficult home life, and four years later, lay dying on a military ship in Manila Bay. A spark of hope encouraged him to pray, *"God, I don't know if my life is to be for evil or for good but I want to live to find out."* He did say his good-byes to this world, but not until he was 105, leaving a legacy worthy of much honor. Grandfather Bud, severely wounded in WWII, was informed by the doctors that he would never run and would find it difficult to walk. Walk he did. Run he did, *"But not real fast,"* he would say with a wry grin.

Amie's grandmother (on her mother's side) was a single mom who raised two kids—mostly alone. Times were tough! But some of our favorite family recipes were born from those days of not enough. They bring a joyful reminder of her hopeful spirit every time we gather around them for dinner.

The common denominator in the lineage of Amie's life was a hope and faith that persevered regardless of the *stuff*. The stuff that happens. The stuff common to us all. The stuff that showed up at Amie's door uninvited. But with the stuff came a promise of hope, and not just any hope.

Amie introduces you to a hope worth embracing, leaning into, and rejoicing in. It's not just a hope that is present when you finally reach your "Matterhorn" mountaintop. It's a hope that springs up from 200 miles away while you're still in the mess of getting there.

You may think I'm partial because Amie is my daughter. You're right. We love many of the same things–Jesus, family, tacos, pistachios, sunflower seeds (cracked from the shell), heart stopping roller coasters, hiking, sci-fi/adventure/murder mystery movies, coffee, journaling, tacos, sushi, theology, (did I mention tacos?), and a good book … including this one.

As you turn these pages you will be drawn in, not only to

Amie's story, but also your own. You'll find yourself identifying with the mess and before you know it you'll find yourself captivated by the message. My prayer is that we all may, with fullness of joy, Hope Fully.

Love, Dad

HOPE FULLY

One woman's journey
to find hope in the mess.

To the one in my story who
taught me what it was to be enough,
cared for me enough to let me go,
and filled my heart with
hope for what comes next.
You were not just a chapter.
You changed the story.

PREFACE

The story I'm about to share with you is my own and its contents represent the facts the way I remember them and the way I felt them. I have been careful to not use names or exact locations and to share the truth to the best of my recollection, but I understand that I may remember the facts in my life differently than those who were party to this story.

I have done my best to be gentle in my delivery of the hard things, but still share those things with you. To be honest, it's difficult to even do that.

DISCLAIMER: I am opening up areas of my life in ways I never would have imagined. Areas I have long kept beneath the covers. *And that means I share some things that **may be triggering** to someone still in the throes of a similar situation. I'm not a therapist and how I coped with my situation may not be how you should handle yours.*

But if being honest and vulnerable on these pages with you will help you to see how God is in active pursuit of your heart, then I won't let my fears stop me. Perhaps through my story you will see Him in your story, even in the middle of your mess. And so I will make a place at my unkept life table for you to sit and share a cup of coffee with me.

It won't be just any old cup of coffee though. I'll get out the French press and the extra cute cups. I'll use only the best coffee beans. I'll set out my favorite lavender honey syrup for you to add in. I'll froth the half-and-half. I'll even make some homemade whipped cream.

In case you haven't yet figured it out, coffee is my love language. I hope it's yours, too.

Speaking of hope. It's here.

INTRODUCTION

LET ME TELL YOU A STORY

"Happy Father's Day to the best dad I know."

The text appeared on my phone lock screen that Sunday morning and I paused. I'm not a dad. I'm a mom. The reality of those words from my friend struck me and the weight of my life as a single parent hit hard.

I was, and I am, both. I'm Mom because I bore them, cared for them, and have raised them the best I could. But I'm also Dad because in this season of our life theirs isn't present and hasn't been for a long time.

Looking back, it's almost silly now. In the struggle of those first years parenting three kids, I had given little thought to my dual role. I was neck deep in surviving and made little room for the hard things to take up space in my thoughts or settle in my heart.

I worked extra jobs to provide for our needs, lived with

my parents more than once to stay afloat. Then I worked even harder at making sure I was raising gracious human beings. Let me tell you something ... those years were flipping hard. I don't just mean they were hard in the way it's hard to get an entire family ready and to church on time. They were extraordinarily hard!

I was a one-woman show. Sure, I had help from my parents, and supportive friends, but I'm the one who had to give an account to Jesus for us. I don't know if you've ever experienced that level of lonely. The depth of lonely where the weight of your home and the responsibility to raise Jesus-loving, kind humans falls only onto your shoulders. But it's an actual thing. That degree of lonely doesn't get satisfied until you allow Jesus to do the work.

There were days when my very best, well-meaning friends wanted to give my kids' poor behavior a pass because "they didn't have a dad." It was these moments that taught me to see the reality of our renewed life in a fresh light.

This life was ours. It was broken, messy, and deeply wounded, but it was equally redeemed and full of unexplainable joy. I remember making a choice that day to live as if our life was lacking nothing. To embrace the broken beauty of our days together and fall in love with this life. To choose hope, and not just a bite-sized piece of it either. But hope overflowing.

Hope didn't come without heartache, though. It was the struggle to stay above the rising waters, the nights of crying out to God, the wanted and unwanted lessons that brought us here. Without those lessons, we would not be the standing testament to God's faithfulness that we are. But we are. It's not despite the brokenness that we stand firm, it's because of it!

Whenever these words have stirred in my heart to write, I waited. I imagined that the story would skip right to the part where I felt whole and life was no longer complicated. But that day hasn't come yet. It isn't the way my life story reads, and it's okay. I also wasn't sure you needed to hear every messy detail of the life that led me to hope if hope was going to be the focus on these pages. While there will be moments I'll spare you the not-so-pretty things, I am now aware that the story isn't complete without taking a step back and bringing you along from the start. You won't truly see His overwhelming goodness if I don't start at the beginning, so I'm in.

I'm in to open up my life vault and share its contents here with you. My story is real, it's messy (and I may ramble some as I struggle with myself to be honest with my words on these pages). But I promise to let the messiest parts of my story out from their hiding place in my heart.

I would say that I don't want to hold back in telling my story, but if I'm being honest, I DO want to hold back. The life I have lived hasn't been the life I set out to live, and parts of it are difficult to share. But if the hard to share parts of my life need to come out from the darkness so that your struggles are in excellent company, then I'll gladly step into the light here with you.

I was a pastor's kid, an only child, attended a private Christian school, and was a good girl. My friends came from the same "well-behaved, Christian kid" mold. We had straight As, we were class presidents, yearbook editors, captains of the cheer team. Our idea of teenage rebellion never amounted to anything more than a few rolls of toilet paper in our teacher's front yard. (Sorry, Mr. T! We only did it because we loved you so much!) I caused my mother much grief once when I painted my fingernails green. She was sure this act would be the hallmark start of my downright rebellious years. It wasn't.

I suppose I know what you are thinking. You read that part about me being a pastor's kid, and you assumed a few things. Sometimes pastor's kids get a bad rap that is often well-deserved, but I just wasn't that kid. From a young age I had a sincere desire to follow Jesus, not because it was our "family business," but because Jesus had my entire heart. I learned as I grew to push aside the person at the pulpit and focus on the message Jesus was speaking to me in that moment. I discovered if I doodled my sermon notes, I could stay focused and allow my heart to hear.

It was there, in those old wooden pews, I learned to write the things God spoke. That's when the books on my shelf full of God's words to me collected. I am grateful that my teenage self took the time to record those words. They are not profoundly written, but they are a living reminder of my journey and a lasting record of God's palpable move in my life.

As I unpack my story on these fresh pages for you, we will visit those words. They are proof that God held me in hope and prepared me for the story He was writing. I've dragged my feet in writing this book because the story was still unfolding, and as I write these words in this moment, I don't feel any different.

God is always moving, and the story is always unfolding. Maybe as I take this journey with you through my past, through hope so full it flows right out of me, I'll land not at the ending I thought I needed, but at a new beginning.

I hope it will bring comfort to your heart to see some of yourself in my words and know that you are not alone. Perhaps you will find grace for the hard things, joy in the unexpected, and hope for the days ahead. But more than anything, I hope you find the story of a Savior in passionate pursuit of His beloved ... and a servant in desperate pursuit of her Redeemer.

Maybe there's a friend in your life who sends you your own version of a "Happy Father's Day" message. I hope you have someone who helps you look at the world in a new light. Or maybe today I'm that friend. Maybe you'll read the kindness of a stranger poured out on these pages and it will change your life too.

Maybe today you let yourself sit in the brokenness just long enough to see it for the gift it is. Maybe today you learn to love the hard things just a little because they are refining you. Maybe today you don't just hope a little.

Maybe today is the day you hope fully.

Let me tell you a story.

I

HOPE WAS

PSALM 33:22

"Let your steadfast love, O LORD, be upon us, even as we hope in You."

MY MOST FAMILIAR PLACE

*A*s the large velvet stage curtains were pulled shut, drowning out the applause and separating me from the audience, I had just one thought cross my mind. Jesus, You are so faithful.

Life, for me, started out a month premature and rather uncertain. A tumor on the base of my spine threatened to take the life I'd been given. If I survived, I'd have to confront the rest of life without a hip socket. The tumor boasted a series of tentacles coming from it that wrapped around my major organs. Even with a poor prognosis from the surgeon, my parents had peace that Jesus was in control.

In fact, my mom was so peaceful that the hospital nurses mistook her calm demeanor for a lack of concern and she had to answer for it. If you knew my mom, you'd know just how much she struggles with worry. For her to not worry when her baby wasn't perfectly healthy was a total Jesus thing. I mean, how do you even explain when someone accuses you of not loving your baby that the worry isn't necessary when Jesus is in control?

The surgery uncovered a miracle. The doctors opened me up to unravel the tumor from my organs, but were met with a surprise. They found that overnight the tentacles had retracted, and the tumor was simple to remove. Two months later I went back in for surgery to remove part of my hamstring so my unformed hip socket had space to grow (did you even know such a thing was possible?). While the surgery went well, the doctor gave little hope that I'd ever walk right. I spent the better part of my first year of life in a body cast and my baby book reads like something out of a sitcom.

Rolled over. *Ten months.*

Sat up. *Ten months, too.*

Gnawed my way through my first pork chop.

Eleven months.

Walked for the first time.

Twelve months.

My parents had genuine challenges in taking care of me in that first year. There are no diapers designed for babies in body casts. No manual written for parents living prayer to prayer in a different kind of caretaker role than they expected. But even in the unknown, hope was alive.

Fast forward three years. It was the fall of 1983, and I was just three-and-a-half years old when I took my first steps into Jeanne's School of Ballet. Not only could I walk just fine, but I'd spend the next sixteen years in that studio dancing hours upon hours every week.

I'd teach classes, clean the studio for gas money, get there early and stay late. I choreographed routines, and wrote and produced a full ballet by the time I was in high school. There were many lessons learned in that musky, sweat-filled room. Even in my youth, I was aware of its value. I learned how to work hard, how to be a wonderful mentor to my students, but also how very much a loving God meets us where we are. I wasn't the baby without a hip socket anymore, but I had created my own set of limitations. I told myself that I was good at ballet, but not great. I didn't think I'd ever be truly great. I felt that way about many things in my life. To be honest, I still do.

Despite those feelings, I poured my life into ballet and God poured His life into me in return. I wasn't the wobbly girl that the doctors said I'd be. And ballet wasn't just my after school hobby. I had a unique opportunity to be a teenager who could speak life into younger girls. It may not have been the popular thing to serve Jesus as a teen, but I hoped I could live in a way that told my students and my peers that it should be. Ballet, and all that came with it, was the ministry of my youth.

It was the week of my final ballet recital and I did a very teenager thing. The phone rang one afternoon at home. I thought my high school boyfriend was calling me on our land line (remember those?) and I tried to run to answer the phone before my mom could. Did I make it? Yes, but not before I met the base of our upright grand piano with the side of my left foot. I'd suffered enough dance injuries over the years to know that I broke something, but my stubbornness won. There was no way I would miss my last recital. Tape wrapped around my foot and revised choreography was the best I could do. Rehearsals were brutal! But that Friday night, I pulled on my point shoes and danced with all I had to give.

The old wood stage beneath my feet was a familiar place and one I cherished. It was there that I grew from a child to a woman and on that final night I was so aware of the grace ballet provided me.

I stood with flowers in my arms, and tears in my eyes as the curtains closed. The only thought filling my mind was how God's overwhelming faithfulness brought me to that place. My life started out on uneven footing, but then God gave me a gift that defied the odds.

My feet may not still dance in that same small country studio, but my heart always will. Hang around with me for any length of time and you'll find me dancing down the center aisle at Target (at the great embarrassment of my children) or in my living room. I hope if you catch me dancing you'll remember the story of how I got there and join me in celebrating the beauty of a faithful God!

The next month was full of final high school things: graduation, graduation parties, last hang out sessions with sweet friends before we went our separate ways. There's something special about finishing high school, but still quite terrifying about moving into the unknown. I accepted a position at a Christian camp for the summer, beginning the day after graduation. The familiar feeling of spending my days in the dance studio or at school with the friends I'd been in class with since the second grade was fading. I struggled to feel safe in the unknown.

Esther came to mind. She left her comfortable home to follow God into a remarkable life, but she didn't know it would end that way. She said, "Yes!" to God's call without knowing the end game. In fact, she approached the king knowing full well that in speaking up she may lose her life.

I will go to the king, though it is against the law, and if
I perish, I perish. Esther 4:16

Was I that bold? Bold enough to let go of all I knew and step into God's calling for the next season of my life? Was I willing to obey Him even if failure was staring me in the face?

I grabbed my newest journal and took a drive that day out to a local orchard to outline all my rational and not-so-rational fears for Jesus. Do you ever understand in your head that Jesus already knows the things you are about to toss His way, but also recognize that you need to tell Him out loud with your own mouth, anyway? Yeah. This was that kind of thing for me and here is what I wrote in my journal during it:

Jesus, I'm moving into a new phase of life, and I'm
scared. I'll be living in a place unfamiliar to me,
unable to circumscribe my quiet, simple life, pack it in
a box and take it with me. I need peace, Lord.

For the next two hours I bantered with God, and when I had said all I could He answered, *"You will always have a familiar place in Me."* That truth came rushing in, filling my heart full of peace and hope for what God had planned for my life. The changing world around me wasn't secure, but God was. He was My Most Familiar Place. Wherever He leads I can go with boldness because He goes with me, always.

I quit questioning God's call on my life in the orchard that day. But I wonder, if I knew then what I know now about the heartache that was coming, would I have said yes to God so wholeheartedly? I don't know. Or would I have thought the fight for lasting hope would come at too great a price?

There's this shift that happens when we are moving from child to adult, where we are suddenly expected to have all the answers. I once had a young friend ask me how to know God's will for their future. She was heading into her last year of high school and everyone she knew was asking her what God wanted her to do with her life.

I wish we would stop asking teenagers, or anyone, this question. Not that it's wrong to think about the future; that's not what I'm saying. But let's teach them to follow Jesus well and live for His glory *today*. And then tomorrow. And the next day.

Have we gained good devotional habits so our foundation is secure? Do we sit in prayer with Jesus and learn to hear His voice so we will recognize it when He calls? I mean, I know school is important, and everyone will need to know how to do math and properly write sentences, but are we teaching our youth that a relationship with Jesus is just as vital to their life for the long haul?

My answer to my young friend was exactly that, "If you do what God is asking you to do today, and tomorrow, and the next day, you will always be smack dab in the middle of His will. You need only to worry about the day you are in and let Jesus take care of the rest."

My Most Familiar Place is the only place I need to be. It's the only place you need to be, too.

———

*I*t's easy to see, now that I'm far enough down the road, why God doesn't show us too much too soon. I think if we knew the gravity of what was to come on the road ahead, it would be hard to hold on to hope. It would be hard to not give up when the waters get too high, too hard to rest in His shelter.

He is good. SO good. He gives us just enough to keep our feet on solid ground, or in my case, dancing in the Target aisles.

HEBREWS 11:1

"Now faith is the assurance of things hoped for, the
conviction of things not seen."

2

JUST SAY NO

*a*n exceptional, retro magnet lives on my refrigerator that says, "Stop me before I volunteer again." I bought it for myself. I'm the first to toss my hand in the air and volunteer as tribute in the *Hunger Games* of real life at the mere mention of someone needing help.

You need someone to run the fireworks booth on the Fourth of July in 110 degree weather? *Me!* You need a coffee delivery because ... well, life hit ... *Me!* You need someone to work the nursery, host gatherings, doodle you a tattoo design ... *me, me, ME!*

I know that Jesus created me with that heart for service. But sometimes I let it overrun my life and my choices in a way that would not be pleasing to Him. I forget to slow my roll and ask myself what it is He wants for me to do. Sure, I can do those things for you and joyfully so. (In fact, I did all of those things I listed up there.) But do I seek first His kingdom in my life? His direction? Do I only say yes to what I should?

Six months into my first year of Bible college, I had already said an exuberant "Yes!" to many things. "Yes!" to concert choir and more than a full load of classes. "Yes!" to a job both on campus and at the hospital next door. I was also roommates with the Resident Assistant which meant many late nights up counseling girls in our quad.

I don't remember feeling overwhelmed at all back then. Having a lot on my plate was not unusual for me. I knew I was right where Jesus asked me to be and that burden wasn't heavy.

I didn't go to Bible college to find a spouse, although that was the joke of the campus. Students would say to the freshman girls as they started pouring into campus housing, "You're here for your MRS. degree, aren't you?" But I suppose finding a life partner is inevitable in that phase of life.

I dated a sweet friend who turned out to be only a friend. Then this guy that worked in the finance department of the college was showing me some extra attention. He had attended high school pastor's kid retreats with me so I knew who he was, but didn't know him well. It wasn't long before he asked me on a date and without even thinking about it I said yes. I remember the twinge of *"Why did I say yes?"* was immediate, but I chalked it up to first date nerves, you know?

One date turned into two and then several months of dating. Next thing I knew, I was engaged and planning a wedding. There were minor things that maybe I swept under the rug, nothing outright glaring or super red-flag-raising, but an internal check that didn't settle in my spirit. My "*Just say, yes!*" mentality failed to consider that sometimes a solid "*No!*" is the right answer. Maybe I was giving myself to the wrong thing.

It wasn't like our relationship was hard at that point. Looking back, I can see that there were signs that this wouldn't be the brilliant, Jesus-focused marriage I had desired in my life (that I *still* desire in my life).

My mom had always had concerns that I'd say yes to the wrong boy. My overwhelming desire to help the people I love sometimes came about at my expense more than their good.

On our first Valentine's Day together, I remember sitting at the top of his apartment complex stairs waiting for him to arrive for our date. He was over an hour late and when I asked what happened he said, "I was out trying to find you flowers."

You might think flowers sound nice, but I'm just not the girl who needs them on a holiday to feel loved. I love flowers and appreciate them, but if I'm choosing between quality time and flowers, the quality time wins every time. I had many times told him that all I want and need is my person next to me. So, in that moment alone at the top of his apartment stairs, I wondered if he was my person. Was that enough to say no to the next date?

The rest of our dating life was non-eventful. There was nothing about our time together that made me draw a proverbial line in the dating sand, but nothing great either. I had counseled many girls in my life to not settle for just any man, and here I was not heeding my advice.

Who was I? I'd like to think it was my kind nature that kept me there, but it was my pride. To leave was to admit it wasn't good, and I excelled at everything I put my hand to.

By the time I admitted to myself that I was unsure, the wedding was a couple weeks away, paid for by my full-time ministry parents who could barely afford it. I blamed my nerves all over again. I didn't take the time to sit in that conversation with Jesus and discover what it was He was saying. I thought after we got married, Jesus would make it all work. He would give me the beautiful union I longed for because I had lived my life for Him and followed the Christian dating rules, right?

The first real fruits of those early "this isn't right" twinges showed up on our wedding night. We married in late spring, and it was arguably the hottest day of the entire stinking year —like well over 104 degrees. Our cake leaned to one side because it was melting, the piano overheated and wouldn't work for the ceremony music, and people were on edge.

I loved many things about that day, but I think somewhere deep down I knew that it was just the things I loved: the flowers, the people standing with us, my family ... but maybe not so much the man I stood across from and said vows to. That is a hard thing to admit even twenty-something years later, and in print for all the world to read.

That night we stayed in a hotel near the airport so we could catch a morning flight to the Pacific Northwest for our honeymoon. He wasn't shy about telling me to get out of my wedding dress the second that we were on the other side of the hotel room door, and he wasn't gentle with me. I told him he was hurting me and his response quick, "This is my night," he said, "you just lay there and take it."

I wish I could tell you he was kidding. He wasn't. I wish I could tell you it didn't affect me. But it did. I felt defeated, used, and everything but loved and adored by the man who, just hours before, had taken vows to love and protect me.

The real irony of it though was that I felt guilty for wanting to have those newlywed feelings because if I'm being honest, I didn't adore him either. The devil was swift to use that moment to speak into my heart the words he liked to let linger there … "You are not enough."

Those first years of marriage were not the beautiful life I had hoped God would swoop in and somehow provide for us. I took my job as a wife seriously, though. I made choices to honor my husband when it would have been easier to deny him that, to take care of him, to love him.

At first, I didn't share my feelings about our marriage with him because I felt like it was my self-made cross to carry. I was the one that said yes when I should have said no. I resolved myself to love him the best I could and to choose joy every day despite my circumstances.

Six months into our marriage, I found out I was pregnant. Part of me wondered why God would allow that to happen in a marriage that felt so broken. Five months later, I miscarried. I remember sitting in my shower crying because my husband didn't like that it devastated me, so he threw a remote my way. He aimed for my head, but it missed and put a hole in the wall of our rented two-story apartment.

Sure he made a joke about it to ease the obvious fear it had caused me. Sure I joked back that he better head to the home improvement store and get what he needed to fix it, but the damage was done … and I don't just mean the damage to the wall.

Heartbroken over the loss, I bought myself some knitting supplies and a "how-to" book and dove right in. I knitted baby things for other people and prayed over those growing families while I did. It helped me to grieve in my time, in my way.

Soon we were pregnant again, and this time I got to carry her and hold her in my arms. I would have two more babies and six more miscarriages over the course of our married life together. Each time the needles in my hands and yarn passing between my fingers brought me through each loss in the way my creative heart needed.

Joy and grief are not opposites. I'm living proof that they can coexist. Even in my deepest sorrow, I held on to joy in the places I could.

The abuse crept in like a burglar at midnight. He would slam his empty water glass in front of me at the dinner table when we had guests. Then he'd toss me a glance that meant he expected me to fill that glass. He "allowed" me to go with friends to the movies if I'd bring him a smoothie home. When I brought it to him after the movie instead of before he hit it out of my hands in front of my friends and told me I was stupid. I didn't clean up the mess fast enough so there were private consequences that night. Job after job let him go. Someone was doing him wrong, and they "didn't deserve" his hard working hours. He then blamed me for our lack of financial freedom.

For many years, I raised my concerns with him. I hoped that we could get some help and learn to do life in a healthy way. And when none of those effort were noticed, I did something different. I tried to create a joyful life for us despite the cloud of abuse I was living under. My photography business supported us and I took care of the house. I planned double dates and built friendships with other couples. At church, I served on my days off and said "Yes!" again to far too many things, so I could feel like I had a life purpose beyond the walls of an abusive marriage.

I thought if I could just do enough, then maybe I'd be enough. Nothing I did, though, was enough to stop the hard things from coming, and the devil used those new wounds to fill my head with questions about my value.

My husband had taken up a pornography habit, or at least I had discovered its existence. He made sure I knew that if I had just satisfied him in the specific ways he wanted, he wouldn't need that vice. I'm trying to be careful in what I share. I don't want to dishonor him with my words, even now, but it's important that you know the outline of the story. I was hurting in a hurting marriage, married to a man who didn't even notice the scars forming. I didn't believe in divorce though, so where was I to go?

Remember how I thought God would honor my faithful life and turn my marriage into something amazing? If only that was how it worked! My effort to serve God did not stop me from saying yes to the wrong thing. It also didn't stop God from transforming my wounds into a story for His good. I ended up with three amazing kids to love and do life with, and that is the sweetest gift Jesus ever could have given me.

———

*G*od does, in fact, promise that He uses all things for His good. And your story, however hard it has been, however desperate it feels in this moment, is no exception. You can hold your head up high and know that there is a day coming when God will get right in the middle of your mess and make it beautiful. He did it for me, He will do it for you, too.

It may not be the same beautiful thing you thought it would be and maybe, like me, you've been saying, "Yes" to the wrong things along the way. So, here is your permission to do something other than say, "Yes" to everything. Here is your permission, if you need it, to just say, "No."

ROMANS 12:12

"Rejoice in hope, be patient in tribulation, be constant
in prayer."

3

SHIPWRECKED AND SHI**ED ON

I'll never understand why the U.S. Navy doesn't set up a recruiting table right smack dab in the middle of the hangar during a squadron homecoming. It's the rush of the fighter jets as they fly over in formation before landing one at a time. The way the pilots emerge from their cockpits, and the sea of people who have gathered to be present for the heroes return home. Experiencing this would stir any heart.

It is moving to see families who have spent months apart reunited in such a grand display of patriotism. I'm sure, if given the opportunity, people would crawl over each other to sign their lives away in service to their country. I think I would have been the first in line!

There was a point in our marriage that I realized we needed a life change if we would have a chance of making it as a family. I asked my husband to consider joining the Navy.

I hoped that the structure of military life would bring the

same structure to our home. We were already living in a town with a large Naval base and so it was easy to join the ranks. It also allowed us to stay in our home and not uproot our life.

I purchased a small dance boutique that year and expanded it into a second location. I loved my little store. The shelves full of pointe shoes waiting to find their way onto a fresh pair of ballerina feet made my heart happy.

More than that, though, I loved the time my baby girl and I spent there together. It was a relief to be somewhere other than home. I was working a few days a week down at the shop and teaching several ballet classes at my old studio the other days.

Comfort followed me through the door every time I stepped from the waiting room into the studio and allowed me to soak in the lessons of my youth all over again. Jesus was always faithful to meet me in that room, and I needed Him at that moment to meet me there again.

Life at home was difficult to navigate. We had suffered two more miscarriages and my husband's violent outbursts were increasing. I was three months pregnant with our second child and one night, he startled me awake. He was on top of me with his hands squeezing around my neck. I fought him off and somewhere in the process he snapped out of the rage he was in and told me he must have been sleeping.

I knew better. I wasn't a stranger to the anger in his eyes when I begged him to stop. But even in the middle of nights like that, Jesus was reminding me of His promised presence. I was living in an abusive marriage with an absent partner, but I didn't feel alone. Jesus was still my Most Familiar Place. He never failed me.

As I put my trust in Jesus for my marriage, my growing family, and my life, He was present. There was so much turmoil and yet I had peace I could not explain wash over me. And so, I kept trying in my marriage. I kept asking for a conversation about our life and our home, but he didn't think we had any problems to work through. His view of our life was the only accurate one.

Soon after, Navy life became a reality. It was early in my pregnancy with our second child when it came time for my husband to sign the last papers and head off to bootcamp.

The weeks flew by and before I knew it, my daughter and I were on a plane halfway across the U.S. for the graduation. We had two days there to explore the city before going our separate ways. My daughter and I boarded a plane to go home, and my husband headed to the East Coast for schooling in his assigned field.

I packed my carry-on light for the plane ride home; just three diapers, wipes, and some snacks. It was only a four hour trip, so I figured we didn't need much. This turned out to be a real rookie mom move!

About an hour into the flight, a blanket of something not so pleasant covered my sense of smell. I realized I would need to bust out a new diaper for my girl sitting in her car seat next to me. I forgot to bring the changing pad, but I did what any good, first-time mom would do and tried to protect her little bum from the dirty plane floor by laying the fresh diaper under her as a substitute.

She was all kinds of wiggly as I unveiled the contents of the diaper, and people aboard the flight were complaining about the smell wafting back from the front of the cabin. I can't say that I blamed them though. It was wretched! I was midway through the diaper change and had just pulled those little velcro tabs around the "prize" when the smell hit my nose all over again.

Poop. The fragrance was unmistakable. I looked down trying to find the source of the smell. My left hand was still gently resting on her belly so she wouldn't roll over. But apparently, in my attempt to keep my baby girl's bum from touching the dirty airplane carpet, I didn't have a good grip on the poop-filled diaper in my right hand. Somewhere along the line, I dropped some poop from the dirty diaper and onto the floor.

Not only had I dropped it, my sweet girl had dug her feet into the poop. She then smeared it all over that yucky carpet I was trying to protect her from and right up my protruding, baby-filled belly. If I told you there was poop everywhere, it would be a gross understatement!

Small, poop-smeared foot prints ran up my pink shirt and I realized just how funny this whole scenario was! The kind stewardess heard the commotion my laughter was causing and saw the predicament I was in. She offered to hold my girl so I could wash out my shirt in the restroom.

I know she was trying to help me, but I also know she was trying to stop me from stinking up the whole airplane. Oh, my! I can still remember the awful looks people were shooting my way, like I had tried to ruin their entire flight on purpose.

Here's the thing, though. My life and that plane ride had much in common; one minute it's traveling along well enough, but then the next minute it's completely covered in poop!

The Navy life treated me with kindness. It gave me a community to get involved in and a built-in support system for the months of deployment when I was caring for the kids on my own. We were coasting through life at a decent altitude for a while.

Our son was born in the spring and a three-month deployment started soon after. It was the maiden voyage of the U.S. Navy aircraft carrier that would travel through an area of South America that had long been closed.

It was a remarkable feeling to be part of history, even if I was just the spouse at home. While my marriage had not improved, I felt proud of us in that season of life. It invested us in something that mattered, and I found a lot of comfort there.

The short deployment took a hard turn. There were many nights Jesus would wake me up to pray. I knew in my spirit that something wasn't right. I knew that my husband was halfway across the world behaving in a way that didn't honor me. That didn't honor the life we had created together.

One day he called me from the boat. They were in port somewhere off the South American coast, and he said that he needed me to deposit more money into his account. My husband explained that he had given all the money he had to a woman with a child on the side of the road.

He knew that my compassionate heart would hear that and be compelled to help, but I had that instant gut reaction he wasn't being honest with me. In our five years of marriage up to that point, I had never seen my husband be compassionate with anyone.

The truth later came out. He had spent the money on a prostitute, and he didn't feel the need to apologize for it. He worked for that money and could do what he wanted with it.

When the deployment was over, we did what any good military family does. We made the six hour drive down to watch the aircraft carrier port and meet our sailor on the dock. With signs of celebration for our sailor in our hands and wearing our most patriotic garb, we gathered with hundreds of other reuniting families.

Watching the ship pull in and dock was something I'll never forget. There were sailors standing at attention in their dress whites lining the massive edges of the carrier. The fighter jets on the flight deck displaying their pilots inside. This outward display of unity, of commitment, and of lives given in service for our freedom all stirred my hurting heart and, for a moment, warmly held it there.

When my husband finally made his way from the ship to us, he didn't stop for that long overdue embrace with his family I saw others locked in. He didn't look me in the eye. He didn't notice the son he left at home three months before was now an infant and no longer a newborn. His words to me in that moment as he walked past us were, "I need to get out of here."

I don't know what it was I expected from that experience, but I went from proud military wife to shipwrecked human being in an instant. My husband would tell you that the moment coming off the boat was not about me. That I had no right to expect anything more from him, and maybe he was right.

I didn't know what it felt like to return home to U.S. soil after three months of living on a floating naval base. But I knew my hope of what could change for us in our marriage and family was not within my human grasp.

However unreasonable it was, I still clung to the hope that Jesus would honor our marriage vows and "fix" us so there could be genuine joy in our life together.

The kids and I had moved into base housing during the deployment. There was an infestation of black widow spiders at our old house (I know, I know, I should have just burned that house down!). In an act of desperation, I called the base to get on the six month wait list for a home.

They had a random home available with no family the right size to fill it, and within twenty-four hours we were all moved. It was a total fluke and a total Jesus thing!

But coming home to that unfamiliar house together was hard in a way I don't have words for. My husband was more removed from us than ever. He spent hours with headphones on playing video games, and the verbal abuse started up right away. It was more intense now and I had to choose my words and actions carefully so it didn't set him off.

My little dance boutique was struggling, and I knew it was time for a change, so I closed up shop and picked up photography as a hobby.

To escape the reality of our life, I would wake up early in the morning, and while the house was still quiet, I'd talk to Jesus. Then I read everything I could about camera settings, lighting, and posing. Those quiet moments were precious to me and gave my heart something to love that didn't hurt me in return.

Before long I had turned our garage into a photography studio and was booking weddings left and right. Having a camera in my hand was natural for me, and for the first time in a long time it felt like I came alive again.

Those early mornings also gave me a space where I could be honest with Jesus about where I was and where I wanted to be. I didn't just find a new hobby in that garage studio, though; I found a habit of prayer, and boy was I going to need it!

There would be four more miscarriages in this season, and in May of that year our third child was born five weeks early. He was so tiny, but so strong! Two days later our next deployment was underway and this time my husband was heading out for a six-month tour on the other side of the world.

Our home life had become so difficult that I remember feeling relief that the boat would take him away again so soon, but then also guilty for those feelings.

I realized in my morning conversations with Jesus that I'd been saying yes to the wrong things again. I said yes to mediocrity in my marriage and to accepting that my husband would expect me to be a dutiful wife whenever he pleased with no regard for my heart. I said yes to a life that was much too accepting of the kind of abuse that makes me want to hide behind the locked doors of that life and hold back in sharing it on these pages.

As I sought Him in prayer in the darkest days, though, Jesus was opening my eyes to see the ways joy was still present in the wreckage.

Joy in every sunrise. Joy in the quiet moments with Jesus. Joy in my children and in the community we were a part of.

I made a choice that day to not let the circumstances of my life steal the joy Jesus provides. I was suffering at the hand of the person who vowed to love me. I desperately wanted to feel a joy in our marriage that just wasn't there. But Jesus loved me first and His joy was all I needed.

That third and final deployment was a fresh wave of difficult. I was caring for a two-year-old, one-year-old, and a brand new baby. To be honest, that wasn't the hard part. I thrived in that role! The hard things came in other ways.

I'd send photos to the boat of our newest baby. All I received as a response was some comment about how big his forehead looked or how "not cute" he was. He never asked about how the other kids and I were doing. The communication waned after that and time passed between phone calls.

That all changed in a moment. I got a call from the boat one morning. It was my husband telling me he was coming home a few days early because someone on the boat had hurt him. The details were intimate.

The words were hard to hear, and that familiar twinge of uncertainty rose inside me. He explained what happened, how he'd be coming home, and how his future in the Navy was not clear.

I wish I could tell you I believed him. I didn't. I believed something happened on that boat, in those sleeping quarters, but the story and his behavior when he got home made little sense in my spirit.

In those quiet mornings with Jesus in the days that followed, I prayed for my husband. I prayed not that Jesus would swoop in and fix us or even fix him, but for the road we had ahead of us to travel, however it looked. Hope lingered, but I let go of what I thought hope could produce in our marriage.

My husband didn't see our struggle, and I could not save our marriage alone. I chose goodness, still served him, did my best to love him where he was. His life, the life I created for him, was happy.

But my world felt under attack from all sides. How was this my life? How long was God going to leave me in these deep waters?

We began making plans to exit military life, and I was heartbroken over it. But I also knew we needed a significant life change again if our marriage and family would survive.

This time we made plans to pick up our life and move up

north. We had dear friends there with a thriving, Jesus-centered family, and I hoped that their influence and companionship might be the thing we needed to find our own way.

We packed the house, loaded the truck, then said our goodbyes. And in December of that year we made the move. Our issues escalated. The violence was becoming part of our everyday life and wasn't just directed at me anymore. He was taking his anger out on the rest of the family.

He threw our Great Dane across the room by her neck, and started spanking our not yet verbal one-year-old when he couldn't say, "Yes, Daddy," as directed.

My husband spent all his waking hours on a computer playing games or on inappropriate websites. He stopped contributing to our life again and left me to take care of the bills and the house.

I was flying or driving back and forth to photograph weddings in our old town that I already had on my books before the move. At the same time, I was trying to build the business again in an unfamiliar state.

I knew something had to give. There was no way we could stay on this path at this pace and survive long term.

One night a few months later, I came home from dinner with a friend and found him on the computer. The screen was filled with some things I wish I could erase from my memory, but for the first time I felt nothing. Not anger, not hurt, not sad. There were no tears to hold back.

I went upstairs and gathered the kids from their beds. We all piled in my bed together and I locked the bedroom door. I knew in that moment that it was time for us to leave.

You would think, given our history, I would have long been looking for the exit sign in our marriage, but that wouldn't be the truth. I believed in marriage, in the vows I took, and the journey to keep trying. I still believe in those things, but sometimes staying isn't the right answer and wasn't the safe choice for my family.

The abuse did not get better. The unfaithfulness did not stop. And I had to leave. There wasn't a single moment that choice felt easy, but on this night I knew that God had given me the release to go.

Our life may have been shipwrecked, but *I was not wrecked*. Jesus had given me the sweetest peace for what was to come. And in that moment, I heard Jesus whisper to my tired heart that it was time to leave the life that held me captive.

You know what, though? It wasn't relief that I felt at all, but an extra responsibility to follow Jesus into the unknown because He had proven He was faithful. I held my babies a little tighter that night as I drifted off to sleep. And as I did, I felt Paul's words in 2 Corinthians flood in and rush over me,

We are afflicted in every way, but not crushed;
perplexed, but not driven to despair;
persecuted, but not forsaken;
struck down, but not destroyed ...
so we do not lose heart.
2 Corinthians 4: 8-9, 16

J may have lived a life in the shadows where I suffered in the depths of abuse alone. I may have waited too long to speak up for myself and to hope for kindness in my marriage. I may have given too much of my heart to the wrong thing. I may have been completely shipwrecked and totally shi**ed on, but I wasn't defeated. My heart found room to hope in the only sure thing there was, the only sure thing there is. Jesus.

PROVERBS 23:18

"Surely there is a future,
and your hope will not be cut off."

4

DREAM A LITTLE DREAM

*T*he phone rang, and I answered. A familiar voice met me on the other end of the line.

It was one of my Bible college roommates and dearest friends. From our first day on campus together, Jesus was at work. We had a lot in common, but more than that, Jesus used our friendship to strengthen our relationship with Him and grow our hearts.

We spent many nights chatting about what most college girls talk about: boys! From my bed on the top bunk, I'd listen to her share. She'd tell me what God was doing in her heart as she spent time with the man she would marry. Without her knowing, I wrote those words in a journal for her. We didn't just talk about boys, though. We talked about our walk with the Lord and the life we felt He was calling us to live. We held each other accountable in our failures and cheered each other on in our pursuit of holiness.

Just before their wedding day, I gifted the journal and its

filled-up pages to my sweet friend and her husband. I hoped it would serve as a reminder of how much a loving God was present in their life together from the very beginning. Several years passed. We hadn't had many opportunities to talk in the years since we left our old college stomping grounds. The distance between our homes and the time that crept by never impeded the bond she and I created in that dorm room, though.

"You don't have to answer," she said, "but I was praying for you this morning and I know there are some hard things going on in your life." She began to list the struggles that I was facing, and she shared with me some of what she believed Jesus had revealed to her in prayer. And she wasn't wrong.

Even from many miles away it was like she had been in our home walking across those dusty, dark wood floors beside me.

Jesus wants you to know it's okay
to leave those things behind.

The words knocked the wind right out of me because I hadn't seen them coming. All at once I couldn't stop the tears, but not because I was being confronted by my present life mess. The tears came because I knew in that moment just how good God was being to me.

Here I was already sure that Jesus had provided me a release to leave my marriage. Yet He still used my friend to calm my heart and remind me I'm not alone. In that moment,

I had been so sure of Jesus' internal words to me. I didn't think I needed the external confirmation. And to be honest, I probably didn't need it right then and there.

But in the days, weeks, and months that followed, I could look back with confidence that Jesus was walking through the fire with me. It comforted my heart to know that Jesus was present in my suffering and sent my sweet friend to encourage me that day. When the hard things came—and they did—I didn't have to wonder if I had done the right thing because there was a confidence that came straight from the One who has planned my whole life and holds it in His hands.

I came home from the grocery store later that evening to find my husband in the living room. He had earphones in, a video game blasting from the screen in front of him, and I didn't see the kids anywhere. They were one, two, and three-years-old at the time and when I asked him where they were he told me they were in the bathtub upstairs. I tried to be calm, but inside I was instantly panicked. They are *alone* in a bathtub?

He said they were being quiet, so I didn't need to worry. But, shoot, it was the quiet that caused me to worry! I told him. He was angry that I would disrespect him enough to question his parenting. There was no discussion because it was of no use. I stopped trying to reason with him because his feelings and point of view won over mine every time. There in my silence, he was winning an argument we never even had.

His response shouldn't have surprised me. We had long done this dance with each other. The dance where he does whatever he wants without understanding the damage he is causing, and I try to mend the wounds inflicted on us as they occur. I was his entire life clean up crew.

This, though, was a defining moment in the choreography of our shattering life. A moment that infused fear into my heart because I understood the gravity of where we were. The majority of his violent outbursts had been directed towards me at that point. His neglect had plagued us all, but in this moment I realized that I couldn't even run to the grocery store for a few minutes anymore and trust that the kids would be safe in his care. Fear set in.

How did we get to this place? How had I allowed violence and fear to be the narrative of my life? And how was I going to lead my family through yet another change?

I had to travel to our old home that weekend to shoot back to back weddings and took the kids with me. Because of the increased violence in our home, I knew it wasn't safe to tell my husband face-to-face we would stay there for a little while. I also knew it wasn't safe to leave the kids alone with him.

To be honest, I needed some time away to process what that conversation should look like. How do you tell the person you'd created a joyful life for that they had abused that life too much to continue?

It was days before I built up the courage to make the phone call. I told my husband we would stay where we were for a while. I needed some time away to process. And then I asked him all the hard questions that I already knew the answers to.

It mattered to me that the answers came from his own mouth. It wouldn't change the fact that I needed to protect the kids and I and create distance between us. But it mattered because I thought it would help his own healing if he could be honest with me for once. *The truth really does set us free.*

Had he made any plans to get emotionally healthy?

Not really. He didn't need to.

Was he going to contribute to financial stability?

He was too hurt. And I was already taking care of it.

Was he willing to help me at home?

He didn't see why I needed that.

Was he going to step up as a dad?

He thought he already was.

Had he been faithful to me?

No.

It's funny that I knew the answers before I even asked the questions and yet they still laid heavy on my already heavy heart. Those first weeks apart required that I process my life in a way I never wanted to do. It required that I lay my feelings, my hurt, and my hopes for a better life at Jesus' feet. It required that I trust that He was present even when I had a hard time seeing it with my own eyes.

I was used to dreaming vivid dreams, but this season of life brought them by the droves. I'm a talker; equal parts homebody and extrovert. There have been countless times that Jesus has used my dreams to speak to me. It's probably because I don't shut up long enough in my waking hours to hear Him.

I'm too busy doing for others to slow down and listen, and

I don't love that about myself. I've struggled with feeling selfish if I take time for myself instead of helping those around me. As I age, however, and wisdom settles in, I'm able to better recognize the need to balance what Jesus is asking me to do for Him or even for myself.

Those years navigating a failing marriage were not so balanced, though. I still didn't believe in divorce. The thought of walking away from my marriage and the fight for it to be good, however right that choice was in the climate it was in, left me feeling like a failure.

So, I let Jesus meet me in my dreams. I tried my best to listen to Him in the night, then let that fuel my obedience when I woke.

The next day my phone rang again. This time it wasn't one of my praying, Jesus-following friends. It was a woman who had worked with me in my photography business. She wasn't a believer, but in our time together shooting weddings, I often talked about my relationship with Jesus and the dreams He had given me. She was a Navy wife too, and the job had taken her family to another state. We hadn't talked in over a year, but that day she picked up the phone.

"Hey, so I know we haven't talked in a while, and I'm not sure why I'm calling you now except I had a dream last night about you. I needed to call and tell you about it."

I was quiet, and she continued, "I remember you telling me about all those dreams you had and I think I had one for you. You and the kids were all in a car together, crossing a state line. A banner flew overhead that said, 'You're safe.'"

I wasn't just quiet anymore; I was speechless. I thanked

her for calling and hung up the phone. It's one thing when someone close to you and close to Jesus steps out in obedience to share something God has put on their heart for your situation. It's an entirely unique feeling to know that God used a non-believer to remind me of my worth.

I realized then that I can trust the dreams He gives me. I hear Him. If there had ever been any doubt before, it reminded me in that moment that I serve a remarkable God who won't leave me wandering alone!

I think about the Sermon on the Mount. How Jesus reminds us He cares for our heart's every need, even in the middle of the deepest messes.

> *Look at the birds of the air,*
> *they neither sow nor reap*
> *nor gather into the barns, and*
> *yet your heavenly Father feeds them.*
> *Are you not of more value than they?*
> Matthew 6:26

It's easy to read those words written so long ago and feel like they are far off, especially in a season of need. We have a hard time getting past our human emotions to see the level of craftsmanship in His care. He is, however, *still* in the business of taking care of our every need, and sometimes that reminder comes from the most unexpected places.

Sometimes it comes in the night to speak to our heart, and sometimes it comes in the dreams of others to fan the flame He kindled in us. Jesus doesn't just tell us we are more valuable than the birds the Heavenly Father cares for, He gives us a roadmap for how to turn that knowledge into action in our life.

Therefore do not be anxious, saying,
"What shall we eat?" or "What shall we drink?" or
"What shall we wear?" For the Gentiles seek after all
these things, and your heavenly Father knows that you
need them all. But seek first the kingdom of God and
his righteousness, and all these things will be added to
you. Therefore do not be anxious about tomorrow, for
tomorrow will be anxious for itself. Sufficient for the
day is its own trouble. Matthew 6:31-34

———

*H*e cares so much for you. You can let go of the grip you have on your life and trust He is in control. He is the one that adds "all these things" to you. I hope in whatever season you find yourself in that you can open your eyes to the unexpected ways that Jesus is present and offering His hope.

I had every opportunity to let fear and worry consume the days after I left our old life in pursuit of what God had for us. But then I'd dream a little dream—or a not so little dream—and know that I was right where He planned for us to be. And that, my dear friend, was enough.

PROVERBS 13:12

"Hope deferred makes the heart sick, but a desire
fulfilled is a tree of life."

5

I WILL FOLLOW YOU

*D*o you know the scene in the movie *Sister Act* when the principal character leads the church choir, full of nuns from the convent, in a rather spirited rendition of the song *"I Will Follow You"*? The song opens with a verse about just how far one will go to follow the one they love. It boldly declares that neither the deepest ocean nor the highest mountain will keep them away.

I think if you ask most women what they want in a relationship, you'll find being pursued somewhere on that list. Can I just tell you that being pursued across state lines by your violent ex-husband does not fall into the category of romantic gestures?

I had made two trips back up to our home in the Pacific Northwest in the months after leaving that life. The first was uneventful. I had a wedding to shoot in the historic downtown district and my best friend braved the fifteen hour car ride with the kids and I so we wouldn't be alone.

We made some great last Northwest memories on that trip; a stop at the local beach, a walk through the old shops in downtown, and one last night in my quintessential craftsman home. The kids were so young then, and I don't have many pictures of our trip, but I will always treasure those moments.

It was the end of a life that I didn't know I'd be leaving, and it was the start of a life on our own that I didn't know would save us.

A month later my dad and I made the trip again, this time in a U-Haul. I planned with a dear friend to go over to our home in advance and remove my husband's handgun. He had agreed to be out of the house while my dad and I were there, but given our history it felt irresponsible to take the risk.

I didn't gather much to take with me: some clothes, a few photos, the kids' beds, the rest of my photography equipment, and the guest bed. That was it. I didn't have time to look through all the boxes of photos of the kids or photos from my childhood in the basement where a lifetime of memories had settled into a home. I was very aware in that moment that the "things" didn't matter. They were just things, and our safety was far more valuable.

Sometimes, even all these years later, I can't remember if I own a crock pot now or if I did in that old life. Do I still have a pizza cutter or did I? My photographic memory sometimes drives me crazy with glimpses of then that don't serve me in finding things now! Most of the time I have to dig deep either in the corners of my memories or in my current kitchen drawers to answer those questions. The life I lived then was not the life I kept living, and often the lines between them blur.

I also rescued our Great Dane on that trip. In the weeks since I had last been home, he had placed her in a small, make-shift kennel filled with mud and feces. The once healthy, 100-pound dog was skin and bones. The neighbor saw us loading up the small U-Haul and came out to be sure I was taking the dog with me. He said she had been put in there a while ago and not fed or taken out. It was heart wrenching.

My dad and I were packing up the last bed when my husband pulled into the driveway. He shouldn't be there, and I felt the familiar ache of fear creep in and settle in my spirit. I knew that going to pick up some of our things to start a fresh life would not go over well, and I was right. He was angry. Like overwhelmingly angry. He demanded we put back what little we had packed into the truck.

While I knew how difficult it was to reason with him, when faced with that conflict head-on I still found myself surprised. Maybe because I am gracious to a fault. Maybe because I hoped for a change that never came. Maybe because I wanted to believe this wasn't my unfolding life.

I'm so thankful for my dad. He explained that we had only taken what the kids and I would need for right now and left the rest. Taking the "things" was not the goal. The only goal was our safety, and in this moment that meant that we could not all live under the same roof.

My husband didn't understand. But he didn't want to understand. That was the truth. He didn't want to hear how our life had been hard for the kids and I. He was happier living with his eyes shut.

As soon as my dad walked outside and my husband and I were alone, the calm demeanor he had attempted to gather and maintain vanished. I came up the stairs from the basement with the last of my photography equipment to find him there, his arms reached out across the walls blocking my exit.

I remember him leaning in as he questioned me. "Who do you think you are? What are you doing trying to leave me?" he said.

I explained that I didn't feel safe there with him, that he had been abusing me for a long time and something had to change. I said all the things I needed to say as gently as I could say them. Looking back now, I wonder if I could have been kinder. There were moments in our upcoming travels through divorce where I wasn't as kind as I could have been, or maybe even should have been. But the well of words that broke free from my broken heart were at least honest in ways I had held hostage before.

I needed him to hear that I never felt valued or cared for. That it wasn't enough to play video games all day, to not be an active member of our family and leave me to pay the bills and raise our babies alone.

I needed him to hear how his comments about my weight and the way he demanded my surrender was demeaning in a way that cut me to pieces. That it wasn't okay for him to bypass the word "no" to force himself on me even though I was his wife.

He begged me not to say more, but I needed him to hear

that I had loved him in the very best way I could despite all of those things. There wasn't an apology that followed. Instead, he said something that told me he didn't understand the life we had been living.

"I thought we were happy," he responded. The words echoed in me. I saw nothing happy about the empty places I'd carried in our life.

"You were happy," I replied, "I woke up every day and chose abundant joy, but there wasn't happiness in our marriage. I served you, not because you deserved it and not because you demanded it from me, but because in serving you, I was serving Jesus. I'm leaving here today knowing I did all I could do to honor you in our marriage."

I know my words stung him. I didn't want to be unkind even in this horrible moment, but the truth was the only thing I could give. The next words out of his mouth changed me, "It's a good thing I don't have my gun right now."

Genuine fear barged in without warning or permission. While he remembers this moment much differently than I do, and is sure he never would have said something like that, the words stuck in my spirit and replayed many, many times.

Still in the stairway with no way past him, I yelled out for my dad even though I knew he was too far away to hear me. My husband dropped his arms from blocking the side door that led outside. I got as far from him as I could as fast as I could. We finished loading the truck, made the Great Dane a makeshift bed in the passenger seat of the rental truck (I wish I had a photo of this. So funny!) and hit the road.

I didn't look back. I didn't talk about what had just

happened. It paralyzed me. How did peace get replaced and how did I not have the strength to keep the fear at bay? Had God not already proven that He was right there in the mess with me?

Six months after the kids and I arrived back in our home state, my husband sold our Pacific Northwest home and followed us there. The *Sister Act* movie soundtrack playing in the background of my life wasn't so much like those moments in a romantic comedy when you think the love story is over. But just then the lead character goes after the love of their life and all is right with the world.

It felt much more like we were being hunted than wanted. I filed for divorce and a few months later it was granted.

The six-ish years of marriage when we all lived together were hard, but I was at least present to protect the kids from his words, his open palms on their skin, and the ease with which he escaped into his own world and out of being part of a family.

Nothing in this world can prepare you as a mother for the day you have to let your abusive husband take the kids you protected without being there to intervene if they needed it. There were many Tuesday and Thursday afternoons from 2 p.m. to 4 p.m. that I dropped them off only to find myself in a heap, crying in my car from the depths of my belly.

The kids were two, three, and four-years-old. I prayed that Jesus would cover their eyes to the hard things and that those visits would be a time of fun for them. But more than anything, I prayed that He would guard their little hearts.

There is a verse in Genesis, just before we are introduced

to Noah, where God says that He wishes He had never made mankind. In my own humanity, it is hard to read those words and not feel as if God is saying them to me, too.

And the Lord regretted that he had made man on
the earth, and it grieved Him to His heart.
Genesis 6:6

I didn't understand how those weighted words could come from a God that doesn't just love, but *is* love! But for the first time in my life, as I was walking through the fire of this situation, I understood so clearly what God was saying to his kiddos in the beautiful world He had made for them. It wasn't that He didn't love them; it was *because* of His great love for them He wished they didn't have to endure the effects of sin on their life.

It was my choice to marry the man that led us to this place. I could sign divorce papers and walk away, but our children cannot do the same. They have to spend their lives in the mess I made, and that is a hard truth to swallow. He is my ex-husband, but not their ex-dad.

Because of that truth, I carried some actual guilt with me for a season. While it still creeps in, Jesus doesn't let me carry that burden alone. He met me in the trenches of life then. And when my life situation causes the mess to rear its ugly head, He still meets me there now.

I'm reminded often that He knows all our steps before we take them, even the steps I'm not very proud to see in the rearview mirror of my life.

I think about King David. He was a man of many sins and had every reason to hide from God. In Psalm 139, however, the song depicts an all-knowing God who doesn't abandon David in his sin, but searches out the sin in his life and loves him deeply through it.

David is so raw with God, admitting his own failures, owning his own stuff, and confident that God is still hemming him in from all sides.

Would you slow down for just a minute and read this familiar psalm and maybe see it in a fresh light? Don't just skim these words, but read them.

Yes, this psalm points to a God who knew the depths of David's being and is present, but it also points to a broken man who gave God the freedom to poke around his sinful heart and lead him in righteousness.

O Lord, you have searched me and known me. You know when I sit down and when I rise up; you discern my thoughts from afar. You search out my path and my lying down and are acquainted with all my ways. Even before a word is on my tongue, behold, O Lord, you know it altogether. You hem me in, behind and before, and lay your hand upon me. Such knowledge is too wonderful for me; it is high; I cannot attain it. Where shall I go from your Spirit? Or where shall I flee from your presence? If I ascend to heaven, you are there! If I make my bed in Sheol, you are there! If I take the wings of the morning and dwell in the uttermost parts of the sea, even there your hand shall lead me, and

your right hand shall hold me. If I say, "Surely the
darkness shall cover me, and the light about me be
night," even the darkness is not dark to you; the night
is bright as the day, for darkness is as light with you.
For you formed my inward parts; you knitted me
together in my mother's womb. I praise you, for I am
fearfully and wonderfully made. Wonderful are your
works; my soul knows it very well. My frame was not
hidden from you, when I was being made in secret,
intricately woven in the depths of the earth. Your eyes
saw my unformed substance; in your book were
written, every one of them, the days that were formed
for me, when as yet there was none of them. How
precious to me are your thoughts, O God! How vast is
the sum of them! If I would count them, they are more
than the sand. I awake, and I am still with you ...
Search me, O God, and know my heart! Try me and
know my thoughts! And see if there be any grievous
way in me and lead me in the way everlasting!
Psalm 139:1-18, 23-24

Can't you just see David up there with the nuns in *Sister Act* singing? I hope when the doubt creeps in for you like it does for me, you remember there is a God who goes before us, stands with us, and hems us in.

There is nothing in David's past that keeps the God of his life from pursuing his heart. And there is nothing in your past that will keep Him from pursuing your heart either.

Fear doesn't have to win, even when the person you fear

follows you home. Instead, hope in the One who pursues your heart and loves you enough to ask you for your heart in return.

———

*T*here is no prerequisite for hope. No score card of your failures being kept. There is nothing you can do to cancel your subscription to His grace. Whatever it is you have done, He will still come running for your heart full steam ahead.

He loved me first. And I will love Him always. I will follow you, Jesus, whatever road it is you take me down. Whatever life it is you so graciously give me to live.

Hey, friend, I've got a secret to tell you. He loved YOU first, too, and He's not done being good to you. So, how about I swing by and pick you up and you join me on that road trip with Jesus? I'll even buy the coffee.

COLOSSIANS 1:27

"To them God willed to make known what are the
riches of the glory of this mystery among the Gentiles
which is Christ in you, the hope of glory."

6

THE SPACE BETWEEN

*M*y daughter was five when she came home from her dad's house one day and exclaimed, "Daddy had a girl in his bed!" She didn't know what she had seen. I was in no hurry to explain it to her, but it was from that innocent childhood remark that I learned about the "new girl" in my ex's life. Our divorce had been final for only ten days. You read that right. *Ten days*. And he was already getting remarried.

It wasn't actually the short amount of time between his ending marriage and his new one that bothered me. He was free to live his life however he saw fit. It wasn't a twinge of jealousy, or hurt, or even anger that hit me. I was firmly on the other side of the "what if I had just tried harder" stage of leaving my marriage. What I was, however, was smack dab in the middle of a unique dichotomy between utter disbelief and actually met expectations.

The space between. The space between divorce and the next thing. Between the freedom of relief and forming fear.

Not even a month before, this man was begging me to stay married to him, promising that he loved me, and unable to imagine how his life would go on without me. I guess sometimes confirmation comes in strange packages. This felt a lot like I'd opened up the Sunday newspaper looking for the funnies and found them right where I'd expected them to be.

On one hand, I understood that some of those pretty words he said to me at the end of our married days were just a bunch of fluff. But I still halfway didn't expect him to display that truth so soon. I mentioned it was just ten days, right? It kind of made my jaw hit the floor.

I called him.

We needed to talk about him taking better precautions around the kids. He told me it was none of my business. He was getting married that week, and if I interfered in his life, he'd [insert expletive here] hurt me.

Oh, man! I was used to the threats, but this took the "my ex is dating again" thing to a whole extra level. He was going to marry someone he just met that lived in an apartment downstairs from him? And there was about to be a woman I didn't know helping to raise our kids. I had no solid place to put the feelings that truth provoked in my heart.

The next couple of years were tough for us all. It's important to me I spare some details of these years for our kids' sake. If they ever pick up this book and read what I've shared here, I want to be sure they don't feel too exposed. So,

I'll do my best to give you a picture of those years without the unnecessary specifics.

We shared custody of the kids. They went to their dad's house (complete with a new stepmom and three added siblings) on the weekends and lived with me during the week. I continued to pray that the kids would be covered by the fun things and not see the hard things. It worked like that for a while.

Over time, however, a corner of the veil began to lift and the kids would share the things they experienced. Things that their little minds couldn't comprehend. What I can tell you is the abuse I knew in my marriage appeared to still be present in his life with the kids. I can tell you there were a lot of things in that home that children shouldn't see. And there were many times that he just flat out refused to care for them which stung in a completely different way.

Knock, knock, knock. My closed fist met the wooden door in rhythm. It was drop off day and the kids and I were at my ex-husband's apartment right on time. The knob turned and the door crept open. He mumbled something about how the kids could come inside and then his eyes met mine. I didn't think he was okay. I was married to him long enough to know what okay and not okay looked like. I watched him navigate a life with a bottle and pills in his hands, but this was a new, different kind of not okay. He appeared to be high.

How could I just leave the kids there with him in that condition? He ushered them inside quickly and closed the door with the kind of force that told me I wasn't welcome on the doorstep anymore. Fear filled my next breath. *How could he take care of the kids in that state? How do I just leave them there like that?*

What happened next isn't something that I am comfortable sharing here out of concern for my kids. I can tell you that there were police officers (many of them), representatives from the legal department, photos upon photos taken, and reports made. It was a tough day on all fronts. And it was many months before the outcome of that day left its home in the dark corners of our life and made its way into the open air.

The space between. The space between uninvited fear and a shattered heart.

My youngest was just four but nearly every weekend, as the visits approached, he asked to stay home from his dad's house. It scared him to go, although he had a difficult time articulating exactly why. It was Fourth of July weekend and only the older two went for the visit. I made the forty minute drive to pick them up with plans to take the kids out to eat. My son got in the car and before I could even start the engine he said, "*Mommy, something bad happened in the bathtub.*"

My momma's heart sank, but I didn't want to make any assumptions about what happened before I heard him out. I won't share the specifics of his experience here because it isn't mine to share, and he is still my little guy to protect.

I will tell you, however, that his words were something a mother should never have to hear from her child's mouth. My heart sank further. As he showed me what happened and explained the details, I knew. *That was no accident.*

I was beside myself. I tried to go to the police, but they wouldn't talk to my son. He was too young, they said. He didn't know what he was talking about. They said they had already talked to my ex-husband who said nothing happened. And that seemed to be all the proof they needed.

You know, I have watched a lot of crime drama on television. So I was expecting to walk into that precinct and have someone listen and then help me help our son, but it just didn't play out that way.

By the time we got home, the covering I had prayed for lifted from the kids and they starting divulging things that they were experiencing at their dad's house.

I also won't share those things here, but it shattered me. *Completely.* The police told me to return the kids to his home on the next visit day. At this point all three kids were begging me not to take them back there. I cannot tell you what it did to me to have to explain to our kids I had no choice.

They were sobbing and holding hands when they walked up to the door and I'll never forget that moment. I thought I had already been shattered, but this was so much more. The leftover fragments of my heart went from shattered to complete dust. I wasn't the only one in pieces. We were all broken.

One byproduct of having called the police to get involved is they required us to use a local facility for exchanges in the future. We just needed to sign up first. If I had known that place existed before, I would have signed up sooner.

I never thought I'd be in a situation where I would need strangers to moderate our exchanges, but what a gift when the kids and I needed it. Knowing I wouldn't be alone in those moments provided my heart space to leave the anxiety of seeing my ex-husband behind and gave me freedom to focus on our kids and their feelings.

Except I never had the opportunity to utilize the exchange center's services.

After I dropped off the kids at their dad's house that day, I went right away to do my intake at the exchange facility. I hardly slept or ate all week waiting for Monday's pick up. He had not let me talk to the kids while they were there, so I was extra anxious.

Something didn't feel right. The phone rang on Sunday and I found the owner of the exchange center on the other end of the line. She was calling to confirm that I wanted to forfeit my week with the kids.

There was a knotted up ball of nerves where my stomach once lived and now I *knew* something was wrong. She said my ex was there that morning with the kids and he said I wasn't coming. He said I forfeited my time. I was beside myself. I had not given up my week with our kids.

After all that had happened in the days before, I would have been there the next morning extra early to pick them up and take them home to safety. I tried to calm myself down and then drove up to meet with the owner of the center in person.

I've never been more thankful that I was good at keeping a journal. That habit filtered into an ability to write the important things of life down and I had done that job well. I had three calendar years full of visit notes I could take to the center and show the pattern of our visitation schedule.

Sitting on opposite sides of a fold-up table, we went through the two year history of our visits. The first thing she had me do was call the local police department to do a welfare check on the kids. As the officer arrived at my ex-husband's home, he called me. He was livid. I wasn't exactly calm myself.

Where are the kids?

I repeated those words over and over again, each time with more emotion than the time before. Somewhere in the middle of my desperate pleas he handed the phone to the officer at the door.

The officer told me to calm down. He was there with my ex-husband who said the kids were fine. He said I should just accept that and move on. But he also told me that the kids were not there with him.

Then where are they? Prove to me they are not buried in his backyard somewhere!

The words came pouring out of my mouth before I had time to notice them forming. The officer said I was too emotional, and he was done talking to me. He said even if the kids were buried in the backyard he wouldn't tell me because I was unable to calm down.

He wasn't completely wrong. I was not calm. How could I be? My kids were not where they were supposed to be and it seemed to be proof enough that their dad said they were okay. It was all the things that a mom's nightmares are made of playing out in broad daylight.

The exchange center owner was as shocked as I was. She looked up at me from her place across the table and said the words that played into my worst fears.

I think he kidnapped your kids.

Those words will stick with me my whole life.

The space between. The space between knowing the hard things are happening and being powerless to stop them.

A part of me died in that moment. There was a loss of control that I didn't have time to anticipate. My kids were missing and I couldn't do anything about it. Tangible fear on one side, and trust in an unseen God on the other. The space between was a chasm so deep that only Jesus could be the bridge. I felt like I had stepped off the edge of that chasm and was falling fast. But there was still an underlying hope that Jesus was on the way to save me, *to save us.* But I wondered if He would make it in time.

I immediately thought about Lazarus lying dead in a tomb. Mary and Martha waiting for Jesus to come, but by their earthly standards He arrived too late. He knew Lazarus was dying, yet He was in no rush to get there. Jesus promised life to Lazarus, but instead he succumbed to death. This confused Mary and Martha. How does the promise of life get fulfilled in death? But then Jesus taught a valuable lesson about the in-between struggle. The struggle where both death and life seem to be claiming victory.

By the time Jesus arrived Lazarus was gone.

And he said, "Where have you laid him?"
They said to him, "Lord, come and see."
Jesus wept. So the Jews said,
"See how he loved him!"
John 11:34-36

Jesus knew the final outcome. He knew that moments later He would call Lazarus out of that grave and back into life, but He still didn't rush the process. He leaned into the right-now suffering and allowed Himself to feel the sorrow of death. Life was coming, and yet Jesus paused to weep. It was a passing moment between promised life and certain death where Jesus allowed the grief to come.

The word "kidnapped" wasn't just a back-of-the-DVD cover description for a movie, it was happening to us. Right here. Right now. I knew the safety Jesus had promised our family. I knew I could trust Him to be faithful again. But I didn't have a script for what would happen next, and that brought along its own dose of anxiety. *All I had was Jesus.* I felt just as lost as the kids, but also full of hope that Jesus, in His goodness, was at work in the unseen places. That I would live to see His goodness.

I believe that I shall look upon the goodness
of the Lord in the land of the living!
Wait for the Lord; be strong, and let your
heart take courage; wait for the Lord!
Psalm 27:13-14

I hope, with all I am, you do not know what it is to have your children go missing, but maybe you've carried a different kind of unbearable loss. Maybe, like me, you are wondering how long Jesus is going to allow you to stay in the lost places. Maybe we rush too fast toward the promised end and miss the refining nature of the process along the way. Maybe it's the in between space where we are meant to learn to trust Him.

I want you to know it's okay to take time to weep. Jesus did. It's okay to sit in your tears and wait for Jesus to come. But when He comes—and He will come—*get up*. Get up and trust that the reason Jesus isn't in a rush is because He knows how the story ends. You will find Him waiting there for you in the space between lost and found. Between this thing and the next thing. Life and death. Joy and grief.

Whatever it is that is missing in your life, and however wide the chasm beneath you … take heart, friend. Your story isn't over yet. And neither was mine.

ROMANS 15:4

"For whatever was written in former days was written
for our instruction, that through endurance and
through the encouragement of the Scriptures
we might have hope."

7

ON THE CORNER OF HOPE & FEAR

*T*he word still echoed in my mind. *Kidnapped.* The woman in charge at the exchange center made a call to an attorney she loved and within the hour I was in her office telling her our story. I know attorneys, like pastor's kids, get a bad rap. But the second I sat down in that burgundy leather chair across from her I knew I was in the right place.

Her words were eloquent, but what was most notable was the kindness with which she spoke them. She told me she didn't care about me, or about a win for the sake of winning in court. She said she cared about the safety of my kids, and she would protect them at all costs. I understood right away what she was saying.

I could imagine how many people sat where I was sitting, with bitterness or vengeance at the front of their lips, looking to hurt the spouse who hurt them first. But I carried none of those expected feelings. I wanted what she wanted; a safe life for the kids.

She cleared her entire day to sit there and comb through our life. I watched her read through three years of emails between me and my ex-husband. I watched her sigh deeply with each passing page. And as she finished she closed the binder with pages full of the hardest things, and looked me right in the eyes and I knew. I knew that in caring for my kids she was caring for me, too.

My mom was there with us. The tears came, lots of them. "I don't know how we will pay for any of this," she said through the sobs. The attorney walked around from behind her oversized mahogany desk and placed her hand on my mom's shoulder. She said just two words.

Jesus provides.

A tangible peace rushed in and filled that room. It was palpable and only Jesus could provide that kind of peace in the middle of the unknown. The attorney scheduled an emergency hearing for Tuesday morning and then turned to me and told me to go find my kids. I didn't know where to start. It was already late in the evening so my mom and I headed home to come up with a plan for where to look the following day.

The exhaustion of the day was quick to set in, though. I fell asleep crying out to God to protect them, hold them, and keep them safe. I woke a couple hours later having had a dream they were at my ex-sister-in-law's home 200 miles away. It was 4 a.m. I woke my parents up and within thirty minutes my mom and I were on the road.

I was accustomed to Jesus talking to me in my dreams by now, but this was still such an enormous risk to take. What if they were not there? What if I wasted all those hours, and we didn't find them?

I met each question with the same response in my heart. Jesus is trustworthy, and He's proven over and over that I can trust the dreams He gives me. In this moment, however, I felt like Peter being called to walk out to Jesus on the water amidst the waves.

This wasn't a smooth sailing business trip to bring home a day's wages worth of fish. It was an act of trust in the living God who calls us into the swelling sea and asks us only to keep our eyes fixed on Him. Wasn't He teaching us to focus on what really matters and to speak peace over the waters that rage around us?

Peter was distracted by the wind and started to sink, but cried out for Jesus to save him. Have you ever noticed that Jesus didn't calm the seas *before* He called Peter into them? The calm came *after* Peter got out of the boat in the middle of a storm! So, like Peter, I followed Jesus into unknown chaos and fixed my eyes on Him.

I knew if the kids were really where I dreamed they would be, I would need help for a peaceful pick up.

Two stops for coffee, as many restroom breaks, and three hours later we pulled into the local police station. Well, truth be told, we didn't just pull into the station. I was so nervous , I backed my truck right into a bright yellow post just outside the station entrance. Thankfully, I didn't cause any damage, but I wondered just how much the police inside would want to help me now!

After a brief sit down with an officer inside, we were back

on the road and headed to our destination. My nerves were wrecked and I had hives from the anxiety taking over my thoughts. A few minutes later, we arrived.

My car met the curb as I pulled up in front of my ex-sister-in-law's home behind the officer. (Clearly, I'm not an amazing driver.) Before I could even get out of the car my ex-father-in-law was in the street and at my driver's side door. He greeted me in his usual manner, dramatically declaring something like "blessings, dear child" coupled with an over-the-top hug that always made me feel uncomfortable. He was quick to make another declaration.

I don't know why you are here, but we want peace.

I'm still not sure if he said that because he didn't expect to be met with peace on my end or because I had a police officer with me. But I was there in the fight *for* peace! Peace for three little hearts that had been hurt by the hardest things.

The questions I had asked myself before flying down a freeway at 4 a.m. were answered. We were in the right place. He told me that I didn't need to come for the kids. That my ex-husband had already explained what happened and the kids didn't need to be found because they were never lost. He implied that my child was mistaken about what happened in that bathroom with his stepmom two weeks before and everything was fine.

I knew better. In my spirit, I knew that if I didn't find the kids that day that I might never have seen them again. I knew the game my ex played. You know, the one where he evokes fear and then makes you think you're crazy for being afraid? I had lived that life long enough to recognize this for what it was and I wasn't as naive this time.

The six bedroom house at the top of the hill wasn't the place you'd imagine kidnapped kids being held. But then again, I knew this wasn't the stereotypical, makes-the-nightly-news situation. That word, *kidnapped*, makes me think of windowless vans in dark alley ways and strangers who take screaming kids against their will, but this wasn't that.

This house on the hill was the home where the people I once called family lived, and they loved my kids as much as I did.

For a brief moment I forgot about my day's suffering, and let peace settle in. For a moment, I was thankful that the people in that home didn't know the kids were brought there by my ex to cripple my heart with fear. And for all the moments after, I was overwhelmed by the goodness of God to give me a dream that lead me to the right place, to this place.

Just past the porch stairs, the oversized, dark brown door opened. Three joyful children bounded down the walkway and into my arms. For the first time in days my whole body sighed with relief. The weight of the unknown lifted. They were safe and happy.

Jesus was so very faithful.

I'm not sure how I managed to keep calm while picking up the kids that day, but I did. The exchange that morning, at the curb where my car brushed the sidewalk, was short and peaceful. But a new chapter of our story was just beginning to unfold.

The drive home wasn't as peaceful. It was just a few hours

until the court order required that I take the kids back to their dad for the usual visit. I would be in contempt if I didn't comply. I made a call to the District Attorney, explained the situation, and told him that we had an emergency hearing in court the next day. Then I asked him if I could have permission to keep the kids until the hearing.

The DA said my ex-husband had already called. That he had heard quite a bit about me from the other side. That he didn't know who to believe, but at this point it didn't matter. The court could handle it from here. He told me he would grant my request to keep the kids with me until the hearing. But he also said if my name came across his desk again, *he would take the kids from us both.*

I probably should have been, but I wasn't afraid of those words. I knew that the kids would be safe that night and that was all that mattered.

It could have been easy to let the lies of the enemy feed the remaining doubts that lingered in my mind. Did I *really* hear from Jesus in my dreams? If I had let those lies take root, I'd never be here telling you about God's goodness!

He gave me a dream in the night that required my unwavering obedience, and because I had learned to trust him in the night, we found the kids that day. They were having a brilliant time with their cousins, exactly where I dreamed they would be, and I'm forever thankful that Jesus spared them from the reality of that situation.

I had a front row seat to see God's faithfulness in action. He was there long before we were, meeting us with His provision. He was so, so good.

So often, when we are in the middle of the downright ugly things of life, it is hard to remember, let alone actually believe, that God truly is good. His goodness isn't just an impersonal description of how He behaves, it is part of His character. He cannot be separated from the good in the same way we cannot separate Him from love. God *is* good. God *is* love.

Understanding the difference between behaving good and being good can dramatically change our perspective. It means I can trust that even when I can't see how, a good God is still using those things for my actual good. Psalm 31:19 says,

Oh, how abundant is your goodness,
which you have stored up for those who fear you
and worked for those who take refuge in you,
in the sight of the children of mankind!

The world doesn't recognize the goodness of God in the hard things the way we do. They don't realize that the "right now" isn't the final destination, and that God has prepared the way. But if we are being honest, and I sure as heck hope that by now we are, we don't always recognize His goodness in the moment either.

It wouldn't be the truth if I said all I had was hope that day we went in search of the kids. It wasn't just my sweet kids that went missing that week. My heart pushed hope aside and was taken captive by fear, too.

While my heart knew full well that God would be faithful, my head let fear have the green light for much of that lengthy car ride. Fear didn't get the final word, though. Jesus went before us and proved again that He is who He says He is.

There was a corner of my mind where hope and fear met. Hope that Jesus hadn't forgotten us, but fear that maybe I had forgotten how to trust Him. But even there, in the unknown places, hope won.

———

I don't know what things have been taken and held captive in your life. I don't know if you feel helpless the way I did, but I do know that Jesus doesn't hold it against you. He knows what it feels like to be helpless and to want to do things His own way.

He was God, in the form of a man on a cross, and while not helpless to escape death, he allowed death to come. In His humanity Jesus cried out to God for any other way, but then willingly went to the cross and taught us how to follow the Father's lead even when our flesh isn't so excited about it. Surrender.

I surrender my *fears*.

I surrender my *control*.

I surrender my *plans*.

I surrender my *whole life*.

Saying the words is easy. Believing them to be true; harder. Surrendering everything to Jesus; the hardest! But the reward is a life where fear and hope don't have to hang out on the corner together anymore. It's a life where goodness wins and hope is an open road.

II

HOPE IS

I PETER 3:15

"But in your hearts honor Christ the Lord as holy, always being prepared to make a defense to anyone who asks you for a reason for the hope that is in you; yet do it with gentleness and respect."

8

THE GREAT EXCHANGE

*D*eny yourself. Take up your cross. Lose your life. When we consider these words from Jesus, we realize that the Christian life isn't for the faint of heart or prosperous in the ways we might expect for it to be. It requires that in a winning world we choose a different way to live … it asks us to lose.

He who finds his life will lose it.

Deny yourself. Take up your cross. Lose your life. Jesus doesn't stop there. He doesn't just give us a hard command and leave it at that. He says instead, *follow Me.*

And with this we discover who it is we will gain in the experience of losing. We will find ourselves in Him. This is the Great Exchange of life; one life for another. All of me laid down, so that I can find life in You, Jesus.

And he whosoever loses his life
for my My sake will find it.
Matthew 10:39

It is an exchange in which we give up the things we want and we desire for the things He wants and He desires. It is in this exchange that we discover our true value and who we are in Jesus.

I want to tell you that by this point in our story I was great at denying myself, picking up that heavy cross, and exchanging my will for His. I was not. Walking into that small, one-room courthouse where another human being would decide the fate of our children is not a cross I carried easily.

The trial lasted two weeks and we passed a lot of our life story around that room. It was difficult for me to process those days. I didn't want to be there, but I knew we had to be if we would ever be safe. I was so thankful for the gift of my attorney and the overwhelming feeling of comfort it brought to know I wasn't facing those days alone.

She had told me early on that she wouldn't lie for me and I didn't want her to. I knew the reason we were in that courtroom was bigger than a fight between two humans who failed in a marriage. I needed help to feel safe again, but our kids were the ones who needed it the most.

There were a hundred lifetimes lived and relived in the ten days in that courtroom. Dredging up the things I had desperately tried to leave behind was vulnerable in a way that

I wasn't prepared for (and was an awful lot like doing it again to write this book!).

At the end of the trial I was given full physical and legal custody. Our kids would have supervised visits with their dad. I came home to an email from him letting me know that he would not be taking the visits. He felt he had a new family to protect. He was sure that the court was wrong about him and I had somehow manipulated the entire system. And just like that, he was physically out of our life.

There's a mixed bag of emotions wrapped up in those words. I felt safe for the first time in a very long time, but the weight of the failed marriage and the reality that the kids wouldn't have a father around was crushing even if I pretended it wasn't. I grieved that loss, not because we missed him or the things we endured at his hand, but I missed what should have been.

Darn it. I should have chosen better. I should still be married because divorce just isn't my jam for a dozen reasons. I shouldn't have to sit in a courtroom and let experts and witnesses testify or tell strangers about our messy life from behind a microphone and an oath to tell the truth. I shouldn't have to protect my kids from their dad. He should be on the same side of that page helping to write a healthy story for our family.

Let that soak in for a minute. I had to protect my kiddos from their own father. There's no roadmap for that life. Heck, and there shouldn't have to be. There was nothing to prepare me for what that life looks like or the emotions I would feel when the reality of it smacked me in the face.

I made a choice coming out of the trial to carry that bigger-than-me cross though and not just carry it, but thrive at it. I started behaving not like the broken family we were supposed to be, but like we were whole because Jesus was faithful to make us so.

I started teaching the kids that our life may look different from others, but it was the life God gave us to live and He only gives us the best things. There is some real comfort in knowing that I don't have to be the one who determines the outcomes of my mess. I serve a God who doesn't change how He feels about me or how He will work all things for my good because He IS GOOD. My life depends on who He is, not who I am!

He is the same yesterday, today, and forever. He gives us what we need, when we need it and we lack for nothing, not because of our efforts, but because of who He is. That is a truth that cannot be taken away.

But if not, He is still good.

This popular phrase floating around the Christian community (and tattooed on at least two lovely friends of mine) comes from a verse in Daniel chapter three. King Nebuchadnezzar has told Shadrach, Meshach, and Abednego that they will be thrown into the fiery furnace if they don't bow down to the god he has made.

If this be so, our God whom we serve is able to deliver us from the burning fiery furnace, and He will deliver us out of your hand, O king. But if not, be it known to

you, O king, that we will not serve your gods or
worship the golden image that you have set up.

Daniel 3:17-18

They tell the king to go right ahead and toss them in because the true God will save them, and even if He doesn't, He is still the only One worth worshipping.

I want to be that mom for my kids. Heck, I want to be that kind of Jesus-loving, God-following, human being for my sake, too! I don't want to bow down to the stigma that comes from being a broken family, especially a broken family in the church. Not then, and definitely not now.

I want to walk into the fire of life with the kind of confidence Shadrach, Meshach, and Abednego did because I trust that God has me covered. That confidence is not gained from my experiences alone, but comes from knowing the God who is trustworthy to provide it.

There were some genuine sacrifices we had to make in the years that followed our trial. While the daily pressure from my ex-husband was no longer physically present, other things crept in to steal our joy. The economy crashed big time and my photography business suffered as a result.

I remember coming home one day and realizing that I would not pay my rent that month. We were already eating a diet of basic essentials like a group of starving college students and I was having a troublesome time letting go of the life we had created. It had been a fruitful season, and I was proud of the on-our-own life we were living.

It was the one and only time in my life that I felt depression creep in. We had to move back in with my parents and I barely remember those days. I remember sitting on the wood floor of our rental house in the corner of the living room while friends helped me pack up our home. I was sinking fast, but in regular Jesus fashion, He gave me a dream.

I woke up with a joy I couldn't explain the next morning and I never again struggled with that kind of darkness, but it gave me a glimpse into the very real world of depression.

I know that my story may not be your story. You may live in that overwhelming darkness with no end in sight and your depression may not be short lived like mine was, but hear this, friend; even there you are not alone. Even there He sees the places of your heart where hurt has taken hold. Even there He draws near.

There's no simple way to let go of your own desires, your own plans, or your own efforts. We like to hang on to them the same way we hold onto those jeans from high school that we know will never fit over our new three-baby-bodies.

Our ways are familiar to us, but His ways are better. I discovered that the more I let Jesus in to replace His ways with my ways, something remarkable took place. The more I let Him in, the more He also came out. I could see clearer, obey easier, and fall in love with the beautiful mess of a life He had given me. I could shout from the rooftops I serve a God who stands in the fire with me.

Less of me. More of you, Jesus.

Shadrach, Meshach, and Abednego were bound and tossed into the fire that was heated seven times hotter than usual. Oh man, do you ever feel like the moment you say yes to doing things God's way the fire gets hotter or is that just me?

The king was sure he had the final word, but when he looked into the fire, he found not three in the furnace, but four!

He answered and said,
"But I see four men unbound,
walking in the midst of the fire,
and they are not hurt;
and the appearance of the fourth
is like a son of the gods."
Daniel 3:25

These three bold, faithful men in the book of Daniel went into the fire bound. They were not bound by their failures, but in their own obedience! And they walked out of the fire *unbound* with the God who saves.

There is something life-giving about that kind of obedience. It's the same obedience that Abraham received from Isaac on the way up the sacrificial mountain.

We tell this story in Sunday school like Isaac was a toddler who would not have understood what was happening. The original Hebrew word used for "son" here in this passage is more closely translated as "lad." Traditionally that word was used to describe an adolescent man between twelve and twenty-five years old.

This radically changes the narrative. It was well within his capacity for Isaac to say no to that trip up the mountain. He was old enough to fight back, old enough to understand, and yet wise enough to obey his father despite the obvious outcome once they reached their destination. Isaac wasn't just obeying his earthly father, but walking in obedience to the God he served.

Isaac was willing to lay down his own life and become the sacrifice God required. What teenager do you know that would carry the kindling up the mountain and willingly become the sacrifice? That's big stuff! God honored the collective obedience of Abraham and Isaac that day and provided a sacrificial lamb as an offering. What a glimpse into the ultimate sacrifice to come!

————

*M*aybe you've been holding on tight to the things you want and you can't see His goodness in your filled-up life calendar. Maybe, like me, you were tossed bound into the fire before you felt ready to worship in the engulfing flames. Or perhaps you have viewed obedience to God as a sort of bondage without seeing the deliverance obedience brings.

And maybe you can take a step back and ask yourself which cross it is you want to carry; the cross you built for yourself, or the cross that leads to unbound freedom granted to you by the God who joins you in the fire?

I encourage you to think about your own life, about

sacrifice, and of the life Jesus has so selflessly given that you might have life in Him. This is the greatest exchange we will ever make.

Deny yourself. Take up your cross. Lose your life. You might just find it.

ROMANS 8:24-25

"For in this hope we were saved. Now hope that is
seen is not hope. For who hopes for what he sees?
But if we hope for what we do not see,
we wait for it with patience."

9

HOPE HAS A FRIEND

 *W*e were in the car on the way to church one Sunday morning. The kids were having a discussion in the back seat about the differences between the amount of storage needed for digital photos vs. digital video files. (Side note: I was an only child and did not understand just how much entertainment was to be had with siblings around.)

My youngest proposed that photos were better to store on the computer because they took up less hard drive space than videos. My older son pointed out, however, that it's possible to just print the photos, then delete them from the computer so that there's more space free for video files.

I was lost in the worship song blasting from the car radio and was only partially paying attention, but then my daughter said something that struck me.

Both take up space. The digital things take up hard drive space, but the printed photos take up real, actual space.

The kids had no idea that they were teaching my grown up heart a lesson beyond their years. All things, in all forms take up space. Wow. Isn't that the truth?

The hours we spend working, complaining, watching TV —all take up space in our day. The clothes overfilling our closets, food filling our pantries, and the things used to fill our homes—all take up physical space. The anger or bitterness we stubbornly hang on to, the love we give away, and the care we provide to ourselves and others—all take up space in our soul.

In the wake of the economy crashing, my photography business had to become more of a weekend gig than a full-time income. It was the beginning of June and my daughter came home from her last day of kindergarten with her school yearbook. I looked through it and wondered if there was a way that I could pour my creativity back into the yearbook staff I was once a part of.

I picked up the phone and called the yearbook advisor. She happened to be my high school teacher when I attended that school. I told her I wanted to volunteer in her class for a day or two and teach the kids what I knew about design and photography. She told me to show up at the start of the next school year so I did. In fact, I showed up every day after that. Next thing I knew, they offered me the job, and I took it.

The first year I taught only two classes; Journalism and Home Economics. The next year I accepted a full-time position adding three grade levels of English, a ninth grade course called Managing Your Life, and two Bible classes to my teaching load.

I once even took on a ninth grade geography class (gasp!). I didn't know a lot about geography so as we studied I cooked food from the countries we were studying and we ate our way around the world. It was fun! I filled my days with learning, my evenings with grading, and the leftover time went to taking care of my family.

One reality of being a single parent is that there's no one else to pick up the slack. There can be a lot of guilt wrapped up in knowing you must give your kids less time than they deserve just so you can keep afloat. I hated that, but I also watched Jesus be gracious to us during it. He was never absent, and He gently filled in my parenting gaps when I was overwhelmed.

I was preparing a Bible lesson for my high school class one evening after the kids had gone to bed. I can't remember what the lesson was about, but I remember God stopping me with these words ...

I cannot fill a need you don't make room for.

I knew the need He was referring to, and I quickly answered Him in my heart.

I'm doing just fine in this alone.

At this point I had been a divorced, single parent for the better part of six years. To be honest, I had become accustomed to the loneliness in a way that made no room for God to step into that area of my life.

My patience became my independence, my independence became my strength, and my strength became my way of life. I loved God deeply, but I was living like I didn't really need Him. In fact, I lived like I didn't need anyone.

From the outside this doesn't look so bad. I made my own money, accepted minimal help, and told people I was actually happy to be doing it all alone. But on this night, God blew the roof right off my self-created happiness. He reminded me of the things He promised for my life before the marriage, the divorce, and the trial.

I know full well that God's promises are eternal and not just for the right now. His promises are not only available and at work in my life when I allow for them to be. But it's also pretty hard to see their presence when I am bent on doing things my own way.

If I want God to be in control, I cannot lock Him out. If I want to love again, my heart's hard drive can't be full of other things, especially my own stubborn choice to forge my own way in this world. My plans are not His plans, and He is the only sure thing.

I'm just going to put this out there, though: lonely takes up its own kind of space. It comes in waves. Sometimes it feels manageable and sometimes it is downright overwhelming. And sometimes it is just a matter of shifting my perspective a little, or perhaps a lot.

Have you ever had someone tell you not to think about something specific like pink elephants only to have pink elephants stomping about in your head? The point is that we can't help but bring to life the things we focus on, whether they live inside the walls of our mind or become part of our actual reality.

I have to acknowledge here that not all loss and loneliness is something we choose. Often it takes root in our lives because of circumstances outside our control and things that aren't our fault. It's not, however, the loss itself that defines us. It is what we do in the face of loss that will shape our life.

Job is my go to guy in the Bible when I'm looking loss square in the eye. That man endured endless suffering all because he would not turn away from the God he served. Job had such resilience!

I have this theory about clustering the awful things in life. Like if all the bad comes in like a flood at once it leaves the other days open for good. In normal life stuff that theory plays out pretty well for me.

You know, like when you accidentally overdraw your bank account because the auto-paid electric bill was crazy high. Or when you get in a fender bender in the grocery store parking lot. But if I was in Job's situation, where the flood never stopped, I'd be asking God, "Dude, what gives?"

Job had every reason to complain; his suffering was vast even compared to the other heroes of the Bible and certainly beyond what we would consider a tolerable amount of distress in our modern lives.

We see that over-budget electric bill, that broken-down car, or find that those concert tickets we were hoping to score are sold out, and we call that stuff tough. This wasn't the level of suffering that Job was facing. He didn't lose one thing; Job lost *everything*. In Job 7:6, he honestly shares his struggle,

> *"My days are swifter than a weaver's shuttle and come to their end without hope."*

He laments about the condition of his life and asks God what he has done to deserve this hardship. Job sees no way to escape the suffering and is sure his life is ending.

Job has no hope. He flat out says it. But isn't this due in part to Job focusing on the condition of his earthly life and all the ways God has allowed him to suffer? There are three other places where Job uses the word "hope" and each time it expresses hopelessness. I feel like Job actually had a lot of tolerance for the hard things, much more than we tend to have.

How often are we quick to mark the situations in our life as hopeless when we haven't even scratched the surface of loss? Finding hope in the deepest messes of life doesn't mean that the mess gets cleaned up. It can simply mean we gain some perspective.

We can look at the mountains in our way, at our individual losses, or at our human inabilities and see nothing to hold tight. Or we can look past those things to the God who created every one of our days, the God who knew we would be here. The God who holds the stars in His hands and holds us, too.

There is a moment in the last chapter of Job when he realizes this very thing.

> Then Job answered the Lord and said:
> "I know that you can do all things,
> and that no purpose of yours can be thwarted. 'Who
> is this that hides counsel without knowledge?'
> Therefore I have uttered what I did not understand,
> things too wonderful for me, which I did not know.

'Hear, and I will speak; I will question you, and you
make it known to me.' I had heard of you by the
hearing of the ear, but now my eye sees You.

Job 42:1-5

Do you see Job's shift in perspective? After spending so much time absorbed in his very real suffering Job had an encounter with himself that leads to an encounter with the living God. He flat out tells God to listen up!

Job recognizes he may not understand what God is doing. He based his understanding of who God is on the experiences of others. But then Job moves his understanding of who God is from his head ("I have heard You") to his heart ("but now my eyes see you").

It wasn't his physical eyes that saw God standing there before him. It was Job's spiritual understanding that broke wide open. He had a personal encounter with the living God! It seems simple, but seeing God's goodness amid immense loss is far beyond our human capacity. When is the last time you had a dreadful day and thought to yourself ...

"Oh, thank you God for this!

To see that He is good in those moments requires that we open the eyes of our heart and let God reveal His truth to us. It requires that we humbly approach Him and let Him get in the middle of our mess to show us who He is.

This is where humility and hope become friends.

Job had to humble himself and accept that the wonderful things he knew to be true about God were a far cry from the suffering he was actually experiencing. It would have been easy to assign those temporal circumstances permanent feelings, but when Job took his eyes off the "right now" he could see God for who He is.

He is a God who gives and takes away. A God who holds us through it all. He is a God who doesn't shy away from bringing us to a place that isn't comfortable, so we can grow in perspective. His good doesn't always feel good, but it is. Friend, it really is.

Sometimes we make choices in life based on what we perceive from others and forget to allow God to be our friend and show us He is faithful. Job had to trust that God would be faithful even though the evidence at the moment spoke to the contrary. I, too, had to let go of the loss I had let take root and allow God to be the One to fill in the empty places.

I didn't have to live with that kind of lonely anymore. Not in the same way I had before. The lonely changed from something that I couldn't escape, to real hope; a hope that God was at work finding just the right thing to fill the corners of my heart.

———

*W*hat will you find if you examine the rooms of your heart? What have you used to filled those spaces? Are you holding on to loss like a familiar friend, onto the things our temporary world says are of value, on to what you desire? Or can you tidy up those places and make room for what God, in His unmatched goodness, would want to give you?

There is joy found when we lay ourselves at His feet and let Him do the uncomfortable housecleaning in our heart. Hope has a friend. That friend could be you.

ROMANS 5:2-5

"Through Him we have also obtained access by faith
into this grace in which we stand, and we rejoice in
hope of the glory of God. Not only that, but we rejoice
in our sufferings, knowing that suffering produces
endurance, and endurance produces character, and
character produces hope, and hope does not put us to
shame, because God's love has been poured
into our hearts through the Holy Spirit
who has been given to us."

TATTOOS & TACOS

*T*he next week I met the most amazing man, and we embarked on a wonderful life together! Just kidding. But I sure had you for a second there, didn't I?

I don't know what I expected to come from the space I'd made in my heart, but no one showed up on my doorstep with flowers, no one dropped into my proverbial lap, or arrived in my life declaring I was their long lost soulmate. Wouldn't that have been something, though?

What I knew, however, was my heart was cleared of the rubble it was housing and I was actively preparing that space for whatever it was God was doing. But life got worse before it got better.

The high school where I was teaching was struggling and unable to pay the staff. I won't go into the details, but that season was difficult in another way. We had two foreign exchange students living with our family and no money coming in to take care of everyone.

Not only was I still showing up to teach a full load of classes, I had to shoot weddings on the weekends to be sure we would have food on the table. Exhaustion had set in, but Jesus met me in my emptiness time and time again. He was so faithful to provide!

The decision to step away from teaching hurt. I loved my job and my students and all the ways that God was moving on that campus. Joy was harder to come by in that season, but hope was just getting a jump start in my spirit. I found myself reflecting on my life and where it was that God would want me to go next.

I was about seven years on the other side of divorce and I made a bold choice to do something new. Something I had been thinking about for quite some time. Something downright permanent.

For many years before this day I had a near-obsession-level love of the ampersand. They are littered about my home in all forms—wall art, on coffee cups, on notebooks, and even a pair of bookends. Any time I'm near a blank piece of paper with a pen in my hand you can bet I'll be doodling one. They covered my classroom walls and I'm willing to bet most of my former students could tell you that the "and sign" is called an ampersand.

There is some debate about where the word ampersand originated and what it represents—and those are fun stories to read—but I'd rather tell you about what it means to me. I was thirty-four years old, and I had lived more life than many of my friends. Since you have been kind enough to read this far, you know most of the story by now, but here's a quick recap.

I was a pastor's kid, ballet teacher, student (more than once), wife, parent, mom to six babies I never met, photographer, divorced woman, single parent, high school teacher, foreign exchange host parent, tutor, yearbook adviser, avid knitter, font enthusiast, and what I haven't yet told you … in the last couple of years I had become a rheumatology patient.

While I had my struggles for sure, I was never very good at seeing my circumstances as a total hinderance … because they were not. Each life challenge is part of my story and however wonderful or difficult that story reads, it is mine.

On a sunny day in the middle of the summer, I did something for me.

I got an ampersand tattoo.

Part of why I love ampersands is because they remind me that life is ever moving, growing, and changing. Yes, I went through a divorce seven years before. But my life didn't end there. Yes, I raised children alone. But they aren't deficient because of this. Yes, I had just lost my job. But a job can be replaced.

Yes, I had days that I struggled and days I felt great. But none of these things meant that I had to wallow, give up, or stop living. There was always an "and" waiting.

I've gone through a divorce *and* I still believe in marriage. I was a single parent, *and* I still got most things done. I was in a career transition *and* it was okay.

Life had not been all rainbows and sunshine, but I was still deeply in love with Jesus. To the average person the word "and" might get passed over, tossed aside, or used without considering its value. Or it may feel overwhelming that life involves both this, *and* this, *AND* this, ***AND*** this. But to me, it provides comfort.

God does not leave me in my circumstances. Where I am now isn't where I'll always be. He is my refining fire and I already know that He will get right in the fire beside me. The &'s of life remind me to keep moving, learning, loving ... & that was all the motivation I needed.

And much to my daughter's (and possibly my father's) dismay, I came home sporting some new artwork on my left wrist.

And the rain fell, and the floods came,
and the winds blew and beat on that house,
but it did not fall, because it had been
founded on the Rock.
Matthew 7:25

When the teaching job ended, it was hard to stomach. I hated leaving my students, my coworkers, and all the ways I felt that teaching was my ministry. I had a friend working at the local chain coffee shop and she mentioned that they might be hiring.

A few weeks later I pulled that green apron over my head, tied the strings in a bow behind me and said yes to an unfamiliar ministry. It was a complete act of dependence on God to even take that job. Pay was minimum wage and much less than I was making as a teacher.

There were many mouths to feed in my house, plus a dog,

a cat, and some chickens. If I had done the math on paper, there was just no way that we could make it on that salary. But I knew Jesus had led me there, and I knew that I didn't need to worry. I was right. We always had enough. Not a lot. But enough. And that was all we needed.

The kids and I adopted a new family motto that summer:

Jesus before tacos. Even on Tuesdays.

If you knew anything about how much we love tacos around here, you'll also know just how much this motto means. Our front door mat proudly displays the words "You better have tacos" to our visitors upon their arrival. It means we choose Jesus over our favorite things even when it seems like we shouldn't have to choose between them.

I mean, there's nothing wrong with loving tacos, especially if there is homemade pico de gallo and guacamole involved, but if I allow myself to love the things of this world more than I love the Creator, I've missed the mark. If I love that job more than the God who provided it, what good is it? If I love my home or the things that fill it more than Him, of what value are they?

My roots grew deep in Jesus in that season. I wasn't any less alone and yet we were thriving. A genuine joy was present, like real joy, even in the brokenness.

As you know, I picked up joy as a habit early in my life. I found joy in knitting baby things for others while I was silently suffering my own loss. I found joy in serving alongside other families at church while my own was falling apart. I found joy in learning to love the broken, because I was one of them. And as my roots grew deep, I also found joy in the waiting for what God was doing next.

Do you know what happens when you have a season of growth? If you've been following Jesus any length of time, or have been a living human long enough to have hit adulthood, you know that often out of growth comes an opportunity for even more. *Translation* ... the stuff hits the fan if you know what I mean!

My phone buzzed in my back pocket. It was my ex-husband. He planned to sign up at the supervising agency and wanted to visit the kids. I'm pretty sure I fell over reading those words.

It had been eight years since our trial and I just never thought I'd be confronted with those words let alone the reality of them happening after all this time. It was hard to wrap my head around. I mean, he only ever picked up a phone to call the kids once a month or so, so why now?

There wasn't a lot of talk around our house of what that kind of change might look like because I just didn't see it coming. I've done my best to honor my ex-husband with my words, especially around our kids.

Their feelings and relationship with him were their own and however difficult it was, I always encouraged them to do what they felt was right with him. They have the freedom to feel however they want to about him and I'm proud of that space I could provide. It wasn't easy. But I held out hope for change and that would allow our kids to experience a healthy relationship with their dad.

But I also couldn't ignore the place we were now. I had,

we had, suffered at his hand and here he was asking for an open door back into those broken places. There were a thousand emotions that flooded in and confronted the places in my heart where fear was hiding.

It felt like I had to make a list of which feelings to prioritize so I could keep my stuff together, you know? So many single parents walking through hard things refuse to be kind when divorced life comes knocking, and I didn't want to be amongst their ranks.

Even in my own desire to be kind and make room for growth, it has not always been easy to let the kids navigate that relationship themselves. They have to make decisions about how much or little they allow their dad to occupy their little hearts. But if Isaac can follow Abraham up a mountain and trust God with his life, then I know I can trust God with their lives, too.

I don't have to tell you that the visits were hard for the kids. Every second and fourth Saturday for four hours they would hang out with their dad and a supervisor in a room filled with things to do.

There was an expectation that they would build a relationship inside those walls, and there was a struggle present in that process that never lifted. A year and a half of visits and the relationship wasn't growing.

There were some hard things that happened in that space, none of which I feel I should share here with you. But know this, Jesus was faithful to be present with the kids and walk through that fire with them.

My momma heart was so proud of the ways they took care

of each other, the ways they took care of themselves, and all the ways they left room for what could be while guarding their hearts from what was. I don't know many teenagers who could do that and do it well, but they did. They still do.

There were more court dates. Too many of them. Visits to psychologists. And court dates again. As I write this, we are still living in this revolving space. Every time I walk in that courtroom, I'm reminded of just how much I have to trust Jesus to hold all the things.

Being divorced and having to navigate all that comes with that title means there are days where I have to dress up to walk into a room with people I hardly know and let another human being decide what's best for our family.

I wish words felt sufficient to describe how hard that is. They don't. The emotions wrapped up in passing the decisions for my family over to someone outside our life are deep. It is, at best, overwhelming no matter the outcome. At its worst it feels like I've handed over the care for my family to someone other than the God I trust to take care of us. That feels incredibly irresponsible and irreverent, but also completely outside my control.

Some days, visits to the third floor of the courthouse in Department 4 end in a way that feels right and some days they bring an anxiety I cannot describe.

But I serve a gracious God, and His grace is so much deeper than the waters that surround my circumstances. His is a hope that will anchor my soul. He promises it! And that is a hope that I can hang onto.

------

*M*aybe you aren't having to fight in court for your kids. Maybe you are dealing with something different.

Maybe you are suffering through so much more than I am. And if you are, I'm so very sorry. The truth is it doesn't matter how bad our life circumstances are because they are not the rubric for our life. Jesus is. He is the Alpha and Omega, beginning and end. And we need only to look to Him for relief on all sides.

When the ugly things of life dig in to steal my joy, I try to remember that the battles of this world aren't fought with ugly things spewed in return. And I've had plenty of opportunity to do so.

The battles of this life are fought on the back of kindness, of gentleness, and of quiet. Those things cannot be taken from me if I hang on tight to them. Kind of like the way I hang on to my tattoos (because hello, they are permanent) and Tuesday taco night (because it will always be my favorite).

PSALM 39:7

"And now, O Lord, for what do I wait?
My hope is in You."

11

JUST SIT IN IT

*H*ave you ever met someone in your life that fits you from the start? Like a familiar pair of jeans in just the right size. Like your favorite comfort food after a hard day. Like the way you can count on the sun to always rise and always set. Like home maybe wasn't just a place anymore, but a person. Have you?

I had been purposeful not to date in the years right after my divorce, and I was determined (or possibly just too darn stubborn) to focus my efforts on life with the kids. I leaned into the lonely for a long time, but about six years into single mom life I opened up to the possibility that I could let love in again.

My friends would probably tell you I took too long to arrive at that place. But it mattered to me that I wait for Jesus to give me the green light to look for something new to fill my heart. I should probably also add that it's likely I waited longer than I needed to. Jesus had been nudging me to make space in my heart for a while, but I didn't want just anything. I wanted something good, and healthy, and right.

I made some not-so-amazing dating choices and just some kinda okay ones; an old college friend that lingered in my life far past his expiration date, a family friend who was more of a friend than anything else, and a man from my church that reminded me daily I deserved better than him (and frankly, he wasn't wrong).

I still wasn't sure that I needed anyone in my life so I didn't work at finding someone great. I just kinda took it in stride. The kids and I were doing okay on our own, and being the independent person I am, I knew to disrupt that life or add to it I'd need someone amazing.

Early in my single mom journey I scribbled some words on a page about the man I thought someday could fill those empty spaces and then I filed that journal on a shelf and never looked at it again.

I wasn't in a place of real pursuit in that area of my life and I had long forgotten about those words. At the bottom of the list was a prayer, a prayer asking God to do the work for me, to plop someone into my lap that would surprise me, and then I asked for the thing that God uses most in my life. I asked for a dream to confirm when the person He intended for me entered my life.

I didn't want to miss it, or dismiss it, or even only halfway give myself to it. That journal didn't come off my shelf again until I gathered the words of my life to comb through in writing this book.

I had forgotten all about that list I made, about the prayer I had prayed, and finding those words on a page from so many years ago brought comfort to my right now heart.

Not too long ago I took a friend up on a dare and joined the world of online dating to prove that there were no real, Jesus-loving men on those sites. I tried it, and went on a few dates here and there, but it just wasn't my jam.

I logged in to delete my account and something kinda crazy happened. I noticed a profile of a man with some cool salt-n-pepper hair and in a moment of abandon I clicked the heart beneath him. He shot me a heart right back.

Next thing I knew we were at dinner on a fall Saturday night at my favorite downtown spot. We closed down the restaurant talking, then walked down the street to another favorite local spot and closed them down, too. One night turned into five months of the sweetest relationship I'd known up to that point.

I got a text from him on a Monday asking me to stop by after work. The second I walked into his living room I could feel the shift in the air, and I knew he was struggling with something. I won't give you the details because they are ours. But he needed to do something for him that meant he needed to walk away from us.

I don't know if you've ever had to walk away from something great before, but it's the deepest kind of hard. We didn't have any troubles or burdensome things in our relationship to latch onto the way you do when you're trying to make sense of the end of something. We were good together.

The months since have been the hardest of my life, and

since you've read this far and have a decent idea of what my life has looked like, that's saying something. Thinking back over those hard things from my marriage, I feel kinda silly saying that enduring this heartbreak has been more difficult, but it has.

It's not even because of what was lost though. I think it's because the other struggles came about because I was too quick to say yes to the wrong things and I had ownership in that mess. Those things came from the outside in, but this … this broke me from the inside out.

This kind of brokenness is messy and deep in a way I never knew I needed to prepare for, but Jesus has met me on the broken road in ways I never saw coming. And that, friend, is the part of the story I want to share here with you.

I have been through other sort-of-breakups since my divorce and while they all had their hard moments for their own reasons, the direction in my spirit was always to let it go and move on. This time, though, was different. There wasn't an immediately clear road before me to travel, but instead a sense that I was to wait on Jesus to guide me.

I took long drives at night to pray, ugly cry, to use real, big girl words with Jesus (I think He understands when I have to toss a curse word or two in there) and then sit in the silence and listen for His voice. A box of tissues that took up residency in the passenger seat was my only company.

At first I focused my prayers on asking for clarity and direction. Jesus had brought this person into my life who had taught me it is safe to receive love, it is safe to follow Jesus into the life He has given us, and it is safe to love wholeheartedly in return.

There was never a moment in those months I doubted I was where Jesus asked me to be. It was the greatest gift that season of life could have given me. We met each other half way. We made kindness, respect, and joy our habit.

I dropped a lifetime of fears at the door and learned how to allow someone to love me in return. It was a lesson I didn't even know I needed to learn, but I did.

So how then could I accept the emptiness from its absence? How could I reconcile in my spirit that this distance isn't honoring Jesus? In the night when I couldn't sleep, in the morning when I woke to a reality that didn't make sense. And in my big girl prayers where I begged Jesus for relief from the work happening in my heart only to be met with the same three words.

Sit in it.

Even in that space where I couldn't settle my spirit I had a deep understanding that God is sovereign and this isn't a mistake. I know on the surface those two feelings seem contradictory, but they just aren't. My lack of peace was His quiet way of telling me that He had other plans for me.

Sit in it.

It's the most blown-wide open my heart has ever felt, and yet the most loved. The most hurt, but also the most sure that the story isn't over and a new story is coming. The most impatient, but also patient in ways I don't expect. To be honest, it's a bizarre feeling to sit in the mess of brokenness and know that it's the place I'm supposed to be. It's preparing me for where He is taking me.

There were moments where life met me in my dreams and held me in hope. But there were also moments where, from a distance, Jesus opened the door to allow me to take care of the heart of the man who taught me to love again. At first it came in a heaviness to pray in the wee hours of the morning. Not only in a heaviness to pray for him, but also for his family.

Jesus asked us to walk away from each other so He could put His arms around their divorced lives. He was bringing redemption to their marriage and family. I'm not saying in my heartache I didn't fight it. And for so long I didn't understand it. But at the same time I leaned in to the heartache and prayed for restoration in his family. I wanted what Jesus wanted, even if I couldn't see the good through my tears in the moment.

I didn't just pray for him. I prayed for her, too. It was *hard*, but I knew no other way to get through it. The more I hurt, the more I prayed for them. The more I asked Jesus to allow me to take care of them from afar. And one morning she pulled up behind me in the coffee shop drive thru where I unexpectedly had an opportunity to take care of their order. Jesus wasn't just redeeming their life together. He was redeeming my heart to serve—even from its driest well. And in the most unique ways.

However it happened, there was something life giving about caring for them from the depths of my own broken heart. Perhaps that seems counterproductive or maybe like I wasn't taking care of myself first, but I know one thing to be true. Jesus designed humankind to take care of each other.

And I've never been sad that I followed that example. My only aim in every moment is to do what it is that He is asking me to do right then and there. And on those days Jesus provided me with a chance to turn my brokenness into a blessing. Healing was starting to grow roots in my heart.

If I'm being honest, I didn't *want* to be hanging out in the middle of this life lesson. In this place where Jesus has asked me to just sit in it. I'd rather be my typical resilient self, brush it off, and move on. It would be *so much easier*. But as I'm obedient to lean into what Jesus is doing here I'm suddenly aware that He hasn't left me alone or without a plan for what's to come.

Today I'm doing the work to embrace a beautifully broken life. The brokenness settles on my heart with the weight of a thousand worries, but suddenly I'm not the one carrying them. Jesus is faithful to bear that burden over and over again. I don't know how long He will ask me to sit in waiting, but however long it is I will.

I have tried to wear graciousness like it was my Sunday best, both in being gracious to him and gracious to myself. I've given myself permission to feel every emotion deeply and permission to not withhold the things Jesus is speaking to me in this season. I've wrestled with understanding why Jesus would seemingly answer my single mom prayers after twelve years only to bring me to a place of brokenness and say,

But not this one, and not now.

One night I was out driving and pulled up alongside a park to pray. We are in the middle of a worldwide pandemic which has shut much of the city down, parks included. So, going through this hard season has presented some added challenges. I spread my arms out across the car, hands wide open, tears streaming down my cheeks as I cried out to God for direction again. He so clearly dropped this question into my heart.

Why do you keep asking Me for the things I've already provided for you? I've asked you to wait. I've asked you to sit in it.

Goodness. He was right. He always is. I pulled out the recent journal I had purchased from the seat beside me and I wrote out a new prayer, a bold prayer. I had avoided asking God for anything in this process because it felt selfish to do so. It felt like I had no right to ask for anything if this is His plan unfolding, even if I didn't understand it.

But then the parable of the persistent widow in Luke 18 came to mind where Jesus says that men should always pray and not lose heart, and in James where he writes that the prayer of a righteous man is powerful and effective.

So I prayed that bold prayer in confidence, and while I won't share all its contents with you, I'll tell you this. I asked at the end of it that Jesus would provide confirmation to my heart by giving him a dream.

We had often talked about how Jesus would use dreams in my life to provide direction, and I also knew that dreams, those types of dreams, were rare for him. I ended my brief journal entry by asking Jesus if I had asked for too much.

I mean, I didn't want to be selfish or needy and at the moment it felt pretty ridiculous to ask for something like that in my prayer. But I also knew that Jesus was in the mess. He was present. He already knew what I needed and where this was going and I could trust Him with my silly prayers. Two days later I looked at my phone to find a text that started with the words ...

I had a dream.

A sweet peace rushed in and pulled up a seat next to the hope in my heart for the first time in weeks. In the made-for-TV movie version of my life, this is where my character would tell you that everything went back to "normal" that day and we had a fairytale ending. But the truth is I am still sitting in the mess of knowing this isn't an accident. I'm sitting in the assurance that Jesus is at work in my heart for a reason I have yet to discover. And that's okay because you know what else I am sitting in?

I'm sitting in trust so big that I can't contain it. I'm sitting in the full assurance that Jesus is who He says He is. And I'm sitting in a place where even my silly prayers are answered and I can move on confidently knowing that it's His voice in my heart leading the way.

I know that Jesus is at work here in the mess. It doesn't lessen the pain, and some days it makes it harder to know I have to stay in this place because He's asked me to, but it also leaves me sitting in the best thing of all....

HOPE.

I have no way of knowing where this road leads and most days I don't need to. (Real talk, some days I just want to know!) But trusting Jesus in this season means I sit and wait. Not that I'm waiting for what I had to come back to me, but waiting for whatever it is that God is preparing.

For the first time, in a very long time, I am confident that He hears the desires of my heart and will not leave me in this mess. I'm terribly aware that there is purpose for the pain and I know that the easy way out won't bear the fruit in my life Jesus is after. He must have something amazing waiting for me on the other side of this mountain and I can't wait to discover it.

Maybe there are places in your life where the road took a turn you weren't expecting and you are doing your best to figure it all out. Maybe the answer for you is to let it go, but maybe it isn't that simple.

Maybe Jesus is asking for you to sit in the mess you made yourself and wait there for what He wants to bring into your life. For you to let Him clear the weeds from the path. For you to be persistent in prayer. Whatever it is He is asking you to do, do it. Do it wholeheartedly. And while you do, remember this....

He has not forgotten you.

He has not forgotten me.

He is not against us. *He is for us.*

And even here, in the waiting.

Even here in the mess.

He is good.

III

HOPE WILL BE

I CORINTHIANS 13:13

"So now faith, hope, and love abide,
these three; but the greatest
of these is love."

12

GRACE IS A TWO WAY STREET

*T*here's a dozen one-way, tree-lined streets in our charming downtown. When I first moved here, it took a while to get familiar with the layout. More than once I turned on my car blinker only to realize in the nick of time that I almost made a dangerous mistake.

I think there have been moments over the last twenty years that I felt like I made a wrong turn. Like I was wandering on a one-way street, stuck in the aftermath of my choices and very aware that I was bringing three precious passengers along for the ride.

I tried to go back to ballet once and signed up for an adult class. The studio was brand new and had not yet installed the full length mirrors that are typically present. I was real glad about that, but not for the obvious reason. I had become accepting of my three-baby-body.

It bore the scars of my life and I wasn't afraid to wear them anymore. I was glad there wasn't a mirror in that studio because the mirror would have told the tale of the clumsy dancer I was now. Seriously. One set of grande plies in and my legs gave out.

Sometimes we don't want to see our life changes so front and center and sometimes those changes happen without our permission. Ignoring them doesn't lessen their impact, though.

I don't remember giving my body permission to gain weight with every new baby I carried, both those that came into my life and those that went to be with Jesus sooner then I hoped. But the weight is also my reminder that I was made for this. God designed our bodies for giving life. So, I'll carry a little more around than I want to with sweet memories of days I've left behind and all the pride I can muster.

There are other truths of our present life that can't be ignored. The relationship between the kids and their dad is hard right now. Hard for them. Hard for him. And hard for me, too. I spent my whole young adult life protecting and preparing their hearts for the day he might invite himself back inside those spaces.

The kids are not even kids anymore. In fact, they are practically adults, and the day I wondered would ever come is here. They are learning to be honest in that space with their dad. To ask him to hear them. To require that he allows them to feel whatever it is they need to feel.

They are mindful of what they should and should not allow into their hearts. They are open to what God would want to do in healing the wounds of the past, but when they are not met with care, the kids are gracious enough to not hold it against him.

I knew my kids were amazing. But this? This is amazing in ways I cannot describe to you. I still carry twinges of guilt that I didn't choose my spouse wisely and they are suffering in the wake of that choice, but I also know that burden isn't mine to carry anymore.

Jesus gathers every last bit of the mess I've made, takes it to the cross, and calls it His own. There's nothing else like it in this life. It took many years before I was able to trust Him with my poor life choices, though. To see His hand in directing my days. Not because I didn't love Him and believe He was good, but because I maybe didn't love *me* so much. I allowed those guilty twinges to color my view of myself.

There were some fun moments along the way in my marriage and for so long I tried to cling to those memories in my head and forget the mess we were in. Because I had a family with him, I felt I owed him forgiveness for the way he behaved. For the abuse. For the lack of leadership in our home. For the indifference toward us as his family. I wasn't wrong about the forgiveness, but I was wrong about the motive behind it.

I thought I was putting my husband and the kids first in setting my own desires for something more aside. I wanted that "God swoops in to save the day" story so much that I ignored the red flags time and time again. If I had just tried harder. If I'd quit being selfish with my own needs. Maybe then things would have ended differently. The guilt wrapped up in the "maybes" deposited on my heart and held me there.

What I've learned in the years since, however, is that wasn't what he needed. My forgiving him to keep the peace and ignoring the nagging feeling I was on the street going the wrong way wasn't forgiveness at all. It was my pride in the way.

I didn't want the label of divorce and so I hid behind the cheerful facade and tried to repave the streets of our marriage. All that did was keep me from understanding my worth. It was many years before I settled those things in my spirit. Even now doubt will rear its ugly head and try to creep into my heart.

I have worked hard to lay it all at Jesus' feet, especially now that their dad's presence in our life is again a reality. I understand more than ever, that to heal and make room for the hard things I had to give myself grace for what was.

Grace for my past.

But there have also been moments when I was so very aware of God's unmatched grace in my life now. For however brief a time, and for whatever reason, God brought me someone to love who showed me that life could be different. That a home filled with joy was possible. He taught me that a family can be blended, but also whole at the same time. It infused hope into my vocabulary, not just in my words but in how I lived.

I'm still crying at the drop of a hat and praying like it's my full-time job. There is a lump in my throat I can't clear and a weight on my chest that doesn't lift. But I'm still not asking for Jesus to just swoop in and fix it. At least not in the way I half-expected to have already happened.

What I *am* asking for is His heart and His understanding, because in my humanity I still can't make sense of it all. I'm asking what it is He wants from me in this season of sitting in waiting. I know He wouldn't ask this of me if there wasn't something for my good waiting on the other end of the grief.

I'm hanging on to hope in the most gracious way that I can, but also allowing myself to feel the depths of sorrow that pour over me. And there are nights, even months later, where sleep eludes me and tears come from the deepest places to soak my pillow. A year ago I would have proudly told you that I'm "not a crier." But today, I'm letting Jesus use the pain of loss to soften me.

I keep thinking about how Jesus must have felt in the days leading up to His crucifixion. He knew His disciples would betray Him. He would have to give His life for a world full of people that didn't even seem to know that they needed saving. There's a moment on the cross when Jesus cries out to His Father asking why He has been forsaken.

Oh, man, can I ever relate. I have struggled with feeling abandoned in all this. I've wrestled with wondering why God would bring the sun only to allow the darkness.

I don't love that I feel that way. I know it's human and even healthy, but I don't want to be anything other than trusting of God and His plan for my life. I want my heart to understand that He knows the ending to this story and it's okay give Him control, even in the middle of my brokenness. And so I have to give myself grace once again....

Grace for my future.

All this time I thought it was my job to provide grace to others. And it is, it definitely is. But it's also my job to provide it to myself. *It's your job, too.*

If you feel like you don't have all the answers, but you pretend to ... *I do that, too. You are in excellent company.*

If you are doing your best to keep your head above water, but still feel like you are drowning ... *You're doing the best that you can and help is coming. I'm watching the horizon for that help to come, too.*

If there are days you cannot, for the life of you, keep yourself together ... *It's okay. Just breathe. Tomorrow is another day.*

And if you wonder if you are enough, even in this season of waiting ... *You are. You absolutely are. So am I.*

I am confident that Jesus will meet you where you are because He's meeting me there, too. He has given us the hope of an eternal inheritance ... an inheritance in which He is the prize. And even in the moments where I wish the prize was the love I both held in my arms and let walk out the door, I know He has not forgotten me. In Psalm 16, David says,

The Lord is my chosen portion and my cup; You hold my lot. The lines have fallen for me in the pleasant places; indeed, I have a beautiful inheritance.
Therefore my heart is glad and my whole being rejoices; my flesh also dwells secure. For You will not abandon my soul to Sheol, or let Your holy one see corruption. You will make known the path of life; in Your presence there is fullness of joy; at Your right hand are pleasures forevermore.
Psalm 16:5-6, 9-11.

The promise of an eternal inheritance doesn't lessen the pain of the living-in-the-right-now emptiness. And, as much as I wish it was, I don't think that it is supposed to. It is the pain that draws us to our knees and asks us to trust Him even in the darkness.

Hope isn't only present in the light. It lives in the mess, too. It wraps us in the warm promise of a life to come where the mess becomes a memory and joy is our treasured friend.

———

A glad heart. A rejoicing soul. A hope for our flesh. A light for the path ahead and joy in His presence! Take hold of these promises and today, as you wander down the road before you, be kind to yourself along the way. Days like today, I need the reminder, too.

Give yourself grace for your past, grace for your future, and know that He is giving you that same grace in return.

Grace is a two-way street.

ISAIAH 40:31

"But they who wait for the Lord shall renew their strength; they shall mount up with wings like eagles; shall run and not be weary; shall walk and not faint."

13

HOPE HAS A NAME

*H*ope. The joyful expectation of good. There's no time frame, no itinerary, no step-by-step instructional guide, but there is an emphasis on the joy present in hope. Hope makes room for there to be joy in the waiting.

There are days in my grown-up-girl humanity, however, that I wonder when the reward for being faithful will come. How long is too long to wait? I know that my Jesus-loving, God-fearing answer should be that it's never too long to wait on His timing and His plans, but we all know in our human weakness we don't always feel up to the task.

Many times over the years I've stumbled my way down the weary road, wishing that it could have been a simple journey that God planned for me. It was not, though. And it's okay.

The irony in all this is that we get so tired of waiting on God that we take matters into our own hands. We exhaust ourselves trying to fit the things we think we need into a box we built instead of taking God at His word and trusting Him to take the lead in our self-orchestrated lives.

When I look back at the words I've poured out here I feel vulnerable. But I can see the story God has written for me up to this point, the lessons I learned along the way, and how my pursuit of Him in the midst of suffering wasn't just for my sanity, but for my actual good.

I knocked down the door of His heart as a youth because He loved me first. I trusted Him in the middle of a failed marriage and the lonely that followed because He's proven Himself faithful.

And I've sat in the mess of waiting ever since because I know His plans are better than my own (even though I might just put up a good argument to the contrary right about now).

Maybe you are not as sure of those things. Maybe you don't see the evidence that God is at work in your situation, and I want you to know that is okay, too. We don't have to see Him at work to have the faith that He is. Hebrews 11:1 tells us,

> *Now faith is the assurance of things hoped for,*
> *the conviction of things not seen.*

We do not hope in vain when we put our hope in the right thing, even if we have to choose it when we don't feel it.

I don't know what areas of your life you hold on to in the absence of hope (or because you're being stinking stubborn) but I know that there is hope to be found lurking somewhere in every situation, even the downright ugly ones.

I know this because hope is not just something we feel, it is the gift of a living God who is sitting in the mess with you writing your story one heartache, one joy at a time.

Since hope is the joyful expectation of good, you can trust that while the good may not feel present in this moment, you can look ahead and anticipate its arrival. Good is coming. Hope is on the horizon. Can you feel it?

I have been thinking about Ruth in the Bible and how her story is meeting me in the corners of my heart like a familiar friend these days. It's a love story of hope, of mercy, and of God's sovereign hand—all born out of a season of significant loss. In fact, her name, Ruth, means "friend" and today I'm sitting with her over a cup of coffee and leaning into her extraordinary life lessons.

Let me set the stage for you. After ten years of marriage, Ruth finds herself without a husband. Her marriage covenant didn't end, however. Ruth remained with her mother-in-law, Naomi, and served her so well that she released Ruth of her bond and sent her out into the world to find a new life.

Here we find the first use of the word "hope" in the Bible. The reference comes from Naomi as she explains to Ruth that she is too old to hope for another husband and have more sons.

It was customary in that time for a woman, whose husband has died, to stay within the family and marry there again, but Naomi knew she needed to release Ruth of that bond. Ruth tried to convince Naomi otherwise. She wanted to remain faithful to the vows she had taken, but God was about to call Ruth to be faithful in a brand new way.

Sometimes we allow ourselves to stay tied to situations that look right from the outside or even feel right at the moment, hoping that our faithfulness will be enough, but we fail to ask God where it is He is leading us.

That word for hope in Ruth 1:12 means to stretch like a rope. It's also used in Psalm 71:5 where Yahweh Himself is called the hope of the godly and in Hosea 2:15 where it's used to show how God's blessing on His land will transform it from the valley of trouble into the door of hope.

What does all that mean for us? It means that hope will stretch us, that hope will take us out of the valleys we are in and open a new door, but more than anything it means that He is the hope we are waiting for. God didn't leave Ruth bound in her circumstances or lonely, and He won't leave me or you there either. He went before her, walked beside her, and gave her the best helpmate. He does not leave us in our loss, in our mess, or in hopelessness.

He is the God of redemption. He exchanges our old trouble for a brand new hope in Him. Our responsibility is to cling to this unwavering hope because genuine hope doesn't focus on the surrounding things. It focuses on the hope-Giver and there is no greater hope than that found in the arms of our Redeemer.

Ruth remained faithful to Naomi, which seems like the right thing to do, but God had other plans. He released Ruth from her bond to her family and she said yes to God's call to step into a new family when it came.

Ruth would marry Boaz who redeemed her family. Together they would be part of the lineage of David and later of Christ. Boaz was Ruth's kinsman-redeemer, and from that came our Redeemer! What a heritage!

I wonder how often we, like Ruth, stay planted where we are because it looks like the right thing to do. I wonder how much of our extended suffering is due to our own stubborn control. If we could see down the road laid before us would we let go easier or is the slow pace also meant for our growth?

I also wonder if we followed Ruth's example and let Jesus lead our lives what would be waiting on the other side? I imagine it would be a life of unfathomable joy! A life where we stop controlling the outcome and rest in Him alone.

There have been many moments in the last couple of months I've wrestled with God, asking Him to examine the deepest places of my heart. To check my motives. To help me carry my seemingly splintered cross, but also to let Him do the heavy lifting. I've leaned into Him in ways I had not done in quite some time.

And maybe some of that is the point here. Maybe I got lazy in my pursuit of Him and needed a reminder of who holds my heart. But maybe it isn't all about me.

Maybe the people who fill my story need that reminder, too. Maybe God is using this season to grow their roots in Him. Maybe they need to walk through the fire of the right now so when God calls them to something new, they can hear Him with confidence and obey.

Twenty years ago I was sitting in my corner college dorm room wrestling with control. I'd been taking charge of my life in a way that didn't put Jesus first. I can't remember the circumstances of that moment or why it was I wrote these words in my journal, but they have often helped me to gain perspective and to recall God's promises when my vision feels blurred.

Even all these years later, it is remarkable to me how God's words can settle in our hearts, make that space their home, and hold us. Those words didn't just give me hope then because they are just as true now. I wrote,

> *I watched intently for the promise*
> *that God spoke so quietly in my heart and when it*
> *didn't come to pass as quickly as I hoped, I got*
> *discouraged. But then I remembered ...*
> *it's not the promise that matters.*
> *It's the One who spoke it.*

Without Him, there is no promise, nothing to hold tight, nothing to pour my heart into. It's not about where I'm going. It's about a day-to-day relationship with the One who is taking my hand and leading me there. Jesus met me in my youth with that promise of His presence and He's meeting me here with it too. His promises are truly eternal. And hope has always been at the heart of them.

I find it so fitting that God uses Ruth and Boaz and their real life love story to introduce us to hope. As I finish writing this book, I'm still sitting in the waiting. I still believe that Jesus has asked me to sit in the mess in this season and trust His lead. I understand the purpose for the suffering even though I don't like it one bit.

Not only that, but we rejoice in our sufferings,
knowing that suffering produces endurance, and
endurance produces character, and character
produces hope, and hope does not put us to shame,
because God's love has been poured into our hearts
through the Holy Spirit who has been given to us.
Romans 5:3-5

Did you hear that? Hope does not put us to shame. In other words, it doesn't disappoint. We like to head straight for asking Jesus to give us this kind of hope when we have neglected to walk through the suffering, when we've not tried to endure. When we've not worked to break through the suffering and allow our character to change.

Hope isn't just a gift. It's part of the refining process in our heart that happens when we rest in Him, when we stay the course, and when we allow a loving God to be our teacher. That hope—His hope—doesn't disappoint. It can't!

I hope that someday (hopefully soon!) I'll get to tell you another story, my real life redemptive love story. But for now I rest in the truth that it doesn't matter what is gained or lost in this life ... in my life. The reward for faithfulness may never look the way I expect it to on this side of heaven. What matters is that I'm putting my expectation in Him.

My soul, wait silently for God alone,
for my expectation is from Him.
Psalm 62:5 (NKJV)

I have always loved this verse. It's one of those times when the comma makes all the difference. Without it, it is easy to read this as "my soul waits in silence". As if quiet patience was already present in the soul. With the comma, however, we can see the plight of the psalmist.

He cries out, "My soul!" and then gives his soul instructions to wait. He's not encouraging the patience already present in his soul, he is reminding his soul to find the patience it lacks in God alone. He is denying the expectations of the flesh and instead expecting that the God of hope and peace is at work in all things.

What matters most as I sit in the mess of today, and the messes of tomorrow, is that hope has a name.

His name is Jesus.

And Hope Himself went in obedience to a cross so that we might live in this life with Him and that is all the reward you or I will ever need. EVER.

———

So yes, I'm both Mom and Dad. Yes, I lived broken in ways I pretended I was not. Yes, I've said yes to many of the wrong things.

Yes, I've let pride tell me I could do it on my own and have walked this life in the lonely places. And yes, my life has been full of the hardest things because of it.

But do you know what else I am? I'm a chooser of joy. I'm broken and humbled in His presence. I no longer wonder if Jesus will bring someone for me to walk with in this life.

He asked me to do the work of making space and I know that He is bringing the right person to fill it. I'm overwhelmed by His goodness. I'm a woman of God filled with the hope that only He can provide.

I'll never hope for anything less than the life He gives me to lead, the family He gives me to love, and the purpose He's created me to fulfill.

All for His glory. All for you, Jesus. ALL OF IT.

So much of me hopes that your life hasn't had to write its story on the pages of loss, of brokenness, or of heartache the way mine has. But if you see yourself in the narrative of my life, I hope you also see a gracious God there, too. Today, and every day for as far as I can see …

I choose to HOPE FULLY.

So, how about we grab that coffee from my favorite local shop, hop in the car for a drive, and you join me in hope?

You, my dear friend, have nothing to lose, and a lifetime of hope to gain.

LAMENTATIONS 3:21-24

"But this I call to mind, and therefore I have hope:
The steadfast love of the Lord never ceases;
His mercies never come to an end; they are
new every morning; great is Your faithfulness.
'The Lord is my portion,' says my soul,
'therefore I will hope in Him.'"

14

HOPE LIVES HERE

*T*he antique, tiger wood, upright grand piano in my living room has traveled this life beside me. We first met when I was seven-years-old. There were years of lessons and hours upon hours spent together. The piano made every life move with me. It's the same piano I broke my foot on in high school while running to answer a phone call. It was there when I needed a place to meet with Jesus in my sorrow. It was there when I needed a place to worship Him with abandon for all He had done. And it's still here this morning as I come before Him again.

My fingers pass over the broken key, half an octave above middle C, before settling in to their place on the worn ivory notes. I'm plucking out a familiar melody. It's from an old hymn playing in the background of my mind this week as I put the final touches on this book and send it to print. It begins with these words:

When peace like a river, attendeth my way,
When sorrows like sea billows roll
Whatever my lot, thou hast taught me to say
It is well, it is well, with my soul
It is well, with my soul
It is well, it is well with my soul!

Peace like a river while still in the depths of sorrow. I have lived those words in the last few months! I've been sitting in the depths of a mess, but peace has travelled with me and become the sweetest friend. My heartache has been replaced with the assurance that Jesus has not been a silent bystander, but a purposeful teacher.

I wondered what the author of this famous hymn faced. So, I looked up the back story. As it turns out, the words for *It is Well With My Soul* were written in 1876, by Horatio Spafford after his already hard life took a tragic turn. His four daughters drowned in a shipwreck on their way from America to Europe. It was as he passed by their final resting place on a later journey, he scribbled down the words to the now famous song. The hymn ends with this:

My sin, oh, the bliss of this glorious thought
My sin, not in part but the whole,
Is nailed to the cross, and I bear it no more,
Praise the Lord, praise the Lord, o my soul
It is well, with my soul.

Horatio Spafford and I have something in common. It was in a state of complete brokenness that Jesus asked me to write. To gather my life story and share it. Words from the last twenty years moved from journals and the pages of my heart onto actual pages. I wrote the first draft in just ten days, but I've spent the last four months rewriting, editing, praying over the pages, and asking Jesus to refine my words.

A funny thing happened in the process. After months of truly sitting in the mess, He gave me permission to get up. The emptiness I felt is no longer an image of loss, but it has become a blank canvas for what He is doing next. Jesus reminded me that the tomb was empty too, and the emptiness is the ultimate symbol of redemption!

So much of what God has promised me over the years is still waiting for His intervention. But as I sat in the mess of loss and replayed that story over and over, I didn't see unfulfilled promises there. What I saw was all the ways God used the "not yets" to grow me. Just like this book, He took me through an editing process, too.

The lies from the enemy that have crept into the corners of my heart and have told me I'm not enough, that my life has been too broken to redeem, that Jesus isn't present in my wandering … they are no longer welcome in my life narrative.

This week my home is empty because my kids are off to summer camp, and so is my stomach as I fast and pray over what comes next. I'm emerging from a season where He asked me to sit in empty places long enough for the story He was writing to become clear, and for Him to be enough.

I cannot deny that Jesus is at work in the most unique ways filling my heart with the right things. The mess He asked me to sit in made room for Jesus to clear the weeds from the path. There was healing in the empty places and He was so very faithful to meet me there. Even in the waiting, His promises are being fulfilled. But even if they are not fulfilled in the way I hope ...

> *Whatever my lot, Lord Jesus, you have taught*
> *me to say, "It is well with my soul!"*

And today I can say, with all the confidence I can muster, He truly is enough. The doors I've hoped would open are open. And He didn't just crack them open a little bit either. He swung them wide open and invited me inside.

———

ope didn't stay buried in a grave after it bore the cross of Calvary, and it didn't stay buried in my heart, either. I want you to know that hope isn't just coming. It's here. And it isn't just here. It's alive!

Hope was written on parchment paper when Horatio penned that famous hymn. Hope was written on the pages of this book as I shared my brokenness with you. But that isn't its final resting place because Jesus became our eternal hope when He walked out of that tomb and into our hearts. And because of that, hope doesn't just join us on the journey. Hope is the journey. My journey to find hope in the mess, provided more than I ever could have asked for as a reward. Hope didn't just visit my heart on the weekends. It moved in. And now I can *hope fully* because …

Hope Lives Here.

EPILOGUE

*I*t occurred to me, as I edited and prayed over these finished pages, that this book may find its way into the hands of someone who doesn't walk this life with Jesus. If that's you, I guess it's possible you haven't even made it this far to read what I'm about to share with you now. But if you did, then listen up. These words are for YOU.

I'm going to let you in on a little secret that may seem strange, and possibly contradictory at first, but hear me out.

I'm not special. I'm not enough.

From the moment that humankind came into existence, and sin separated us from the Creator, God began writing His redemption story. He didn't wait for us to be good enough to receive His gift of salvation. Jesus didn't just come in the middle of the world's mess. He came in the flesh to live among *our* mess too. To suffer beside us. To show us what love in action looks like. To save us. God's redemption for His creation was Himself!

You may have been thinking as you combed through the chapters of my life that the hope I held onto was unique to my faith. Maybe you think hope doesn't exist for you in your situation. But it does. Jesus left the ninety-nine to run after the one. And today that one is YOU.

You heard me. I'm not special, *because Jesus is chasing after your heart the same way He chases after mine.* We get equal treatment in this relationship. Always. And it's His pursuit, His love, that causes hope to spring up from the ashes. I guess that makes us both special, though. Doesn't it?!

I'm not enough, either, *but He is.* Jesus is faithful to fill in my gaps, look my mess square in the eye without even a flicker of fear, and call me beautiful. He sees your beauty where you are now too, and loves us both enough not to leave us there.

It wasn't just *His* story of redemption that spanned the time from the garden to the cross. It wasn't just *my* story of redemption written on these pages. He also wants it to be *your* story. There's a place in your heart that God wants to fill to overflowing. Maybe you already feel the vacancy in your heart that He's asking to fill. You can trust Him to move in. He's a good tenant, a gentle teacher, and a loving Father.

And today He is knocking gently at the door waiting for you to offer Him a place at your table. He won't beg you or force you, but you'll know that tug in your heart when it comes. If you have been waiting for an invitation to lay down your life and let Jesus have your heart … this is it, friend. He is calling you into a life with Him.

But now thus says the Lord, He who created you,
O Jacob, He who formed you, O Israel: 'Fear not, for
I have redeemed you; I have called you by name, you
are Mine. When you pass through the waters,
I will be with you; and through the rivers, they shall
not overwhelm you; When you walk through fire you
shall not be burned, and the flame shall not consume
you. For I am the Lord your God,
the Holy One of Israel, your Savior.'
Isaiah 43:1-3

*S*aying "Yes" is simple. Get out your big kid words and be real with Jesus. Tell Him all the things that scare you to death about serving Him in this life and then lay them there at His feet. Invite Him into the corners of your heart and then really let Him in.

You've got this! I'll be here to walk this road with you, too. Seriously! This life was meant to be shared and I can't wait to share it with you. Please connect with me if you are choosing to let His hope hold your life today. Scroll ahead a couple pages and you'll find links to my little corner of the internet. We can hang out there. Until then, I'll be praying for you. I may not know you yet, but Jesus does! Would you take a moment to pray for me, too? We are still in the fight around here. *Hope always, sweet friend. Hope always.*

A NOTE FROM THE AUTHOR

Thank you for taking the time to read my book! I am humbled and overwhelmed at the amount of support I've received— so many of you have reached out to tell me that you saw your own story inside of mine. That you allowed hope to become your friend.

To be honest, I needed your words of encouragement to forge ahead when fear tried to consume the publishing process. Writing a book isn't for the faint of heart, and I certainly needed that added dose of courage from those of you who held me up when I wanted to give up. Thank you.

Would you take a moment to use your words for good once again and help me get this book into the hands of others in need of hope?

Go ahead and pass that hope along!

ACKNOWLEDGMENTS

My family. For all the ways you supported this endeavor and were willing to share your story on these pages. I'm the lucky one around here.

Deloise. I didn't want the circumstances that led us to you, but our life is richer because you are in it. You are a gift to us. I would say that I'll forever be in your debt for what you've done for us, but I know you wouldn't let me. Thank you.

Ashley. I knew when you stopped our conversation on the way from one work meeting to another to ask me if we could pray, that you were my person. Thank you for driving me around the city to pray when I wasn't strong enough to drive myself quite yet.

Stephanie M. Thank you for wishing me a Happy Father's Day all those years ago. You changed my life and didn't even know it. Although I kind of think you won't really want the credit.

Glenn and Jessica. For spending your evenings with these words (and my kids at youth group!) and pouring your wisdom into them both. What a joy it is to serve beside you.

Phoebe. For holding me in prayer so faithfully and checking in on me when I felt completely broken. I'm so grateful for your heart and friendship. Who knew when you booked me for photos all those years ago that we would be serving Jesus together now. You are loved, sweet friend.

Stephanie U. You didn't know asking me if I had thought about writing a book was confirmation of what Jesus was already speaking to my heart. Thank you for being the first set of eyes on these words and for pushing me to not hold back.

Taiko. Thank you for the encouragement and investment in our friendship from the moment it started. And for sharing your love of writing with me, too. You were honest with your feedback and also became my cheerleader! I needed both things more than you know.

Hope*Writers: Chelsea, Katelyn, Taiko (again!). Finding local people to stand with while we navigate the world of sharing our stories in print has been priceless. I love that our Sunday afternoons together provide a safe place to land, coffee to enjoy around the table, and enduring friendship.

Lynn (S.C.), Dawna, Katie, Alia, and Stacey. You are all a part of this story and your friendships have spanned the whole of my life. Thank you for being the hands and feet of Jesus to me in my darkest days and in more ways than I have room to share here.

Mrs. G. You were my "other mom" and I am better because of it. Thank you for teaching me to give all I had to many worthwhile endeavors, but always to Jesus first.

Benton S. For being the little sister I never had. Your strength, wrapped in the sharpest wit, is a beacon of hope. We have not walked the roads we wanted, but I'm so proud of you.

Nancy S. For believing in me always and teaching me more about life and Jesus than you ever did about math.

Emily, Bethany, and Rhonda. For letting me into the girl group and doing life beside me ever since. Our adventure dinner dates are some of my favorite moments … ever.

Lucy, Dalia, Becca, and Amanda. For the flowers, walks around your neighborhoods, ice cream runs, and long night drives. You loved me when I wasn't sure I loved me, and I hope you felt loved right back.

J.J. For literally walking beside me and leading with honesty and integrity. Here's to adventures in hope, all for His glory.

ABOUT THE AUTHOR

Amie is Mom to three of the least teenager-y teens on the planet, a Jesus-lover, and joy-chooser. She lives in a cute city, in her own home with the kids, two dogs, five chickens, and a cat (reluctantly), where she survives on hope and (possibly way too much) coffee … preferably a french-pressed blonde espresso roast with homemade whipped cream and a dash of cinnamon powder.

You can find more of her work and connect with Amie at any of the social media outlets linked below, or on her blog at www.amiebeth.com

facebook.com/amiebethwrites
instagram.com/amiebethwrites